# Planet Police

## NEVER A DULL MOMENT POLICING THE STREETS OF BRITAIN!

## Natalie Vellacott

# Onwards and Upwards Publishers

Berkeley House
11 Nightingale Crescent
Leatherhead
Surrey
KT24 6PD
United Kingdom

**www.onwardsandupwards.org**

Printed in the UK by 4edge Limited.

| | |
|---|---|
| ISBN: | 978-1-910197-85-1 |
| Typeface: | Sabon LT |
| Editors: | Peter King / Hannah Settle |
| Graphic design: | LM Graphic Design |

# About the Author

Natalie was raised in a Christian home in West Sussex, England to parents Keith and Kim Vellacott, along with her two younger siblings, James and Lauren. She professed faith in Christianity at a young age but fell away from God at seventeen, having just been baptised.

Natalie subsequently spent many years living a worldly lifestyle before being decidedly converted at the age of twenty-three.

Career-wise, Natalie joined Sussex Police as an officer when she was just nineteen. Within the police she worked in many departments including Uniform Response and Patrol, CID (as a detective), Child Protection and Internal Investigations. After her conversion to Christianity in 2005, Natalie continued to work for Sussex Police and was promoted to Sergeant in 2009.

Natalie found it increasingly difficult to be a Christian in a secular work environment and her focus was gradually changed to mission work. She took part in street evangelism in her spare time and spent many hours sharing her faith with colleagues at work. In 2011, Natalie felt that God was calling her to apply for a two year commitment on the Logos Hope Christian missionary ship. She applied for a two year career break from Sussex Police, which was granted, and was subsequently accepted for the Mission after initially being told she might have to go to Afghanistan instead!

Natalie fulfilled her two year commitment on the Logos Hope, as well as publishing her book, "They're Rugby Boys, Don't You Know?"[1] in August 2014. Natalie's debut true account details her experiences working amongst street teenagers abusing solvents in Olongapo City in the Philippines. As a result of her experiences, Natalie developed a heart for the people and country of the Philippines and subsequently moved to live and work there as a full time

---

[1] Published by Createspace; ISBN 9781502994929

independent missionary evangelist in December 2013. She is currently serving with Cubao Reformed Baptist Church in Metro Manila, working with homeless people and teenagers who abuse solvents.

Natalie is the founder and a trustee of the Christian charity "Olongapo Christian Help and Hope" which operates in the UK providing funding for street teenagers in Olongapo and the surrounding areas. Natalie maintains her connections with the "Olongapo boys" and continues to support various related projects with charity funds.

Natalie often uses her personal story as a living testimony of the hope that can be found only in Jesus, inspiring others to seek Him as their source of hope. She seeks to help people find assurance in God's promise of eternal life through the verse in Romans 10:9: "If you declare with your mouth, 'Jesus is Lord,' and believe in your heart that God raised him from the dead, you *will* be saved." (NIV, emphasis added)

Dedicated to the officers whom I
served with and those who continue
in service.

# Contents

Planet Police

# Introduction

On one otherwise uneventful day in August 2011, I cleared out my locker, packed up my things and walked away from Worthing Police Station for what turned out to be the last time. I had decided to take an extended two year career break after nearly a decade of service as a Sussex Police Officer. I say "nearly" a decade as when my Certificate of Service arrived, it was endorsed "9 years and 11 months"; I had missed the ten year milestone by just a few days.

I soon managed to put this final annoyance behind me to focus on what lay ahead. My new vocation was to be somewhat different to my previous life as I joined the Logos Hope Christian missionary ship for two years. My police colleagues remarked that they didn't expect to see me return and in my heart I knew that my focus had been changing for some time; the career break was more of a safety net than anything else.

This book, however, is not about my missionary experiences, some of which can be found in my previous book "They're Rugby Boys, Don't You Know?". I have written this book to address a curiosity amongst the general public about the police. During my first two years as a missionary, I have discovered that whenever it was established that I was a former "cop", this seemed to become much more interesting than anything I could do or say as a missionary! Whilst unfortunate in some respects, like the time when I was passionately imploring a group of Christian Filipino girls not to waste their lives but as soon as I had finished speaking they just wanted to know whether I had ever handcuffed or arrested someone, I do understand their curiosity; I had the same fascination before I joined the police.

This account is by no means an exhaustive record of events throughout my service. Any officer will tell you that enough things happen throughout a police career to fill many books. This is written as an overview of the significant events that stand out in my mind. It addresses the questions most frequently asked of me: what is the worst incident you dealt with, the funniest, the craziest, the most serious, etc. I have also included some personal life experiences outside of the police environment, as these impacted the way I dealt with things at work.

By the end of my service in 2013, I had worked in most major departments including Uniform Patrol and Response, Criminal Investigation Department (CID), Child Protection Team (CPT), and Professional Standards Department (PSD/Internal Investigations), as well as some lesser known roles. I had investigated every type of crime from traffic offences, thefts and minor assaults to burglaries, rape and murder.

All of the stories are true to my best recollection although I have omitted names and some details for obvious reasons. I hope you will enjoy travelling with me on this journey of nine years and eleven months with Sussex Police.

# CHAPTER ONE

# Rebellious Streak

From the earliest time that I can remember I wanted to be a police officer. I had a strong sense of justice and fairness, and as I grew older, I developed a keen interest in courts, investigations and legal processes. I began reading true crime books in my early teens and discovered I had a fascination with criminal minds and the motivations for criminal offences. Sometimes I was appalled by details of the more vicious and gruesome crimes but my interest was fuelled by a desire to see the perpetrators of these acts apprehended and punished according to the law. My highest ambition was to be a criminal detective in the UK's police force and my best efforts were poured into this.

In my view, studying for its own sake was pointless and I was only motivated to do enough to get where I wanted to go. In the same vein, if someone asked me to do something, I wanted a reason before complying, which often caused conflict. People, especially those in authority, didn't like to be asked questions; they just liked to be obeyed.

As you have probably gathered, I was a pretty rebellious high school student. I resented being transferred from my mixed middle school to an all girls' school in a different town and wanted people to know it. I wore the wrong uniform, spoke German in my French class and vice versa, was cheeky to the teachers, all of which frequently resulted in my being sent out of the class. I engaged in other antics mainly for the entertainment of my fellow students; a friend paid me fifty pence to fall off my chair on one occasion because the class was so boring. In my defence, I did have one teacher with a short temper who resorted to throwing objects across the classroom and another whose solution for those requiring slightly more guidance was to laugh dismissively and tell them to "force yourself to understand". I was the class clown for a few years although I never did anything really serious requiring a suspension, probably because my family were Christians and I had been brought up to know right from wrong.

At times people found my behaviour troubling, and I was often conflicted within myself, as I loudly proclaimed my Christian beliefs in RE class only to be sent out of French for deliberately tilting my watch to reflect the sunlight into the teacher's eyes. It wasn't that I didn't believe the things that I had been taught, I was just having trouble translating this into practical Christian living. Creating havoc in the classroom just seemed to be so much fun that I didn't really see it as "sinful".

Somewhere along the way I became distracted from my childhood dream of being a police officer, possibly at the age of sixteen during my two year stint at college where I studied A Levels in Law, History, and Government and Politics. Whilst at college, I worked thirty-four hours a week at a local mushroom factory alongside my course. Due to working full time, and therefore having access to money, I was one of the first in my college year to pass my driving test and to purchase a car. Later I wondered whether this was a wise decision on the part of my examiner, who had remarked that I had nearly knocked over an old lady (whom I hadn't even seen) as I left the test centre and that I should never stop in the manner that I had on re-entering the centre. My instructor also frequently fell asleep during our lessons and sometimes forgot even to put the L-plates on the vehicle.

Because I was working practically full time alongside my college course, I didn't have much time for a social life. One of my college tutors remarked that he would never usually condone or recommend a student working so many hours but that I was making it work, handing in my assignments on time and passing my exams. This tutor also passionately implored us to seek the best for our future lives by studying hard, frequently referring to past students who had not heeded his advice and were now working full time at Argos and McDonald's. I should add that I have no problem with people working at either of these places but I guess my tutor's point was that it wasn't many students' ambition when starting college.

My history classes were the best, in entertainment terms, as our tutor seemed completely oblivious to what was happening in his classroom including being seemingly unaware of one boy who was always high on some kind of substance and constantly talking on his mobile phone. The lessons were across the lunch period and every week a group of us piled into my car as I drove at top speed into town to buy a McDonald's during the lunch break. We were always late to return to class and traipsed in, eating the remnants of our takeaway, expecting to be berated, but our tutor just carried on talking without acknowledging us or even noticing that we had returned.

It was whilst studying Law at College that I decided I liked the idea of earning good money and wielding power in a courtroom, in addition to working for fairness and justice; so I amended my long-term plan to "Lawyer" instead of "Police Officer". I was probably also influenced by several court room dramas I had watched. Of course, I would be a prosecutor, not working on behalf of the defence, which justified the decision in my mind.

After college, I began studying Law and Criminology at a good university, which will remain nameless, but found on arrival that I was unable successfully to disengage myself from the alcoholic whirlwind of "Freshers' Week". The campus was vast and widely spread out, making it difficult to find the various buildings for my classes. I hadn't realised until this point that I was sick to the back teeth of exams and essay writing having recently finished college. When I did manage to locate my classrooms and attend my lectures, one of my teachers seemed to be suffering the effects of some sort of substance abuse. She riled all of the students by suggesting a preposterous theory about a well-publicised child abuse case. Maybe her purpose was to engage us in a debate, but the subject was in poor taste at best and downright offensive at worst.

The final straw was when I realised that the course material for my Law classes was exactly the same as the A Level course I had just completed at college. By this point I was having doubts about having gone to university in the first place and was really missing my friends and family who lived four hours away. In the end, I made the very tough decision to drop out of university after just six weeks and attempt to join the UK Police Force as had been my original intention.

As I was preparing to leave, I was visited by a police detective investigating the theft of one of my store cards that I hadn't even been aware was missing. I expressed to him my ambition to be a police detective one day. When I told him I was from Sussex, South East England, he laughed and told me not to bother as it would take me twelve years to become a detective in that part of the country. He encouraged me to consider relocating to have a better chance.

I arrived back in Sussex feeling a bit of a failure and wondering if I had done the right thing by dropping out of university at such an early stage. However, Sussex Police had just started recruiting so I applied immediately. The next six months were a dark period as I slipped into hopelessness whilst waiting desperately to hear back from the police. I worked several low-paid jobs including packing greetings cards in a warehouse and potting heavy plants outdoors for twelve hours a day. At the latter, I lasted just two days before quitting due to exhaustion. Next, I decided to have a go at telesales as my brother James had become one of the best agents in the country earning more money than I had ever earned. I thought it would be easy but I quit after just two hours, having taken the customers' abuse far too personally.

So I became officially unemployed for the first time in my life and I hated it. I was nearly climbing the walls with restlessness and boredom and had very little money to top it off. I had received various additional forms from the police which had been promptly filled in and returned, including my initial medical details. This caused a bit of a stir as I was summoned to see my family doctor who was concerned that I had potentially made a misrepresentation by omitting information. Apparently I had had a high temperature fit when I was eighteen months old and nearly died; how I was supposed to remember that, I have no idea.

After five weeks of this misery I was at the end of my tether, when finally I received a more official letter and information pack, inviting me to attend an initial two day assessment. This was to include various verbal and written tests, a presentation, a fitness test and an interview. I was so relieved and knew that I must pass these tests for the sake of my sanity as there was no contingency plan.

# CHAPTER TWO

# Initial Assessment

Details of the preparation required for the two day assessment were contained within the pack I had received. I read everything eagerly and for the first time in my life sought to prepare properly. The first task was to prepare a five minute speech on a topic that I found interesting. I was to deliver this to an audience without notes and to be asked questions about it. I chose the subject of one of the true crime books that I had read recently. It explains how a person can be born with certain chromosomes that give them a propensity towards violent crime. In this particular case the experts demonstrated the materials that made up this man's body were a rare and deadly combination making him almost certain to commit seriously violent crime. They didn't go as far as to say that this meant that he wasn't responsible for his crimes but the implication was there. It was definitely a fascinating topic.

I was also to complete a five minute "bleep" test involving running back and forth between two points, trying to hit the points before the bleep. The time between the bleeps decreases as the test progresses, so the person running has to speed up. I grew to detest the sound of these bleeps as I developed an irrational fear of this test, having failed it a few times. In preparation, I set up a similar test in my back garden and practised for many hours to ensure I would make it.

The big day arrived and I duly attended the assessment at Sussex Police's Headquarters in Lewes. I was extremely nervous, partly because I was just nineteen, and sitting in the lobby in the reception area I could see that most people in the group to be assessed were thirty years and over, although there were a few my age. On speaking to them, some had impressive records of study and many years of previous work experience. What did I have? I was a very young university drop out. But I was also nervous because becoming a police officer had been my lifelong ambition and there really was no back-up plan. Everything was hanging on this two day assessment.

Our group bonded well, encouraging and motivating each other, which made the whole experience easier for me as a lot of the tests were group discussion based. I scored really badly in these exercises as I tended either to dominate the conversation or not say anything. I wasn't very good at getting others involved or listening to different points of view; I just wanted to get the job done. I did better in the written exercises which tested observation and written skills, but I was still surprised at my comparatively low scores. Of course, we were only given the results at the end of the two day assessment so we had no idea how we were doing as we went along.

My presentation went really badly as I was so nervous I was shaking and couldn't remember the speech I had so carefully memorised. I ended up reading it haltingly from the piece of paper, as beads of sweat formed on my face. The panel of judges didn't help in this respect as they didn't smile or offer any encouragement, and I felt a bit silly talking about the obscure subject that I had chosen: "Inside the mind of a serial killer". In hindsight it would have been better to talk about something less complicated instead of trying to impress the panel by speaking about a police related topic. I heard afterwards that one girl had spoken for five minutes about her cat!

The second day arrived and with it came the dreaded fitness test which had been changed to an assault course instead of the bleep test. I was relieved to hear this in one respect, as it was only three minutes long instead of five, but on the other hand I had practised for the bleep test. I decided that it was worse than the bleep test as instead of all of us running together in a line, we had to do the course one at a time with everyone else watching. The assault course was when things really went wrong; in an effort to prepare myself for the physical test, I had quit smoking only two or three days before. I struggled through the test becoming increasingly breathless as the effects of my smoking habit made my lungs wheeze and I stopped to cough a couple of times. The last requirement was to drag a dummy body around a pole which I did slowly, feeling as if I was about to collapse and sure that I was out of time. Actually, I passed the test by just one second but I was advised by the instructor that I needed to sort my fitness out. Considering it was a straight pass or fail with no second chance, this was a bit too close for comfort.

The saving grace of these two days was my interview. I knew that based on everything else I was doomed to failure: the tests had been so much harder than I expected. I was fortunate that one of the two officers interviewing me was a detective. I spoke about my childhood dream to join the police and one day to be a detective. I was honest about my mistakes at university and at other points in my life; I think they appreciated my honesty. They said that many candidates were not as forthright. I was asked if I wanted to add anything at the end and I said "Yes, this is something that I really want to do and if I'm given the chance I will give 100%." The detective smiled and said to me, "That came across." With that one remark I knew that I had made it. I was grateful to him as it meant that whilst some of my group were fretting and stewing as we waited for the outcome, I was fairly confident that I had made it; I didn't think the officer would have encouraged me otherwise.

Later, we all sat in a room waiting for our names to be called. In the end they just called two guys out individually and then informed the rest of us that we had all passed. They said it was the biggest number in a single assessment group to pass. We had really helped each other through the process. I was elated and definitely ready to begin a new chapter in my life.

# CHAPTER THREE

# Sussex Police Headquarters, Lewes

After successfully passing the two day assessment, I was given an official start date of May 14th, 2001. The probationary training period for a new police constable was two years. The first two weeks were to be at Lewes HQ, then there would be four months away in Ashford, Kent at the police residential training school, from which we would travel home for weekends.

On my joining date in May, I drove excitedly to HQ and joined the other new recruits for the start of our two week training. Unfortunately, I was unable to sleep during the first few days and became restless and irritable, wondering if I had made a big mistake. The other recruits were mostly older, with more life experience or university degrees, and I felt intimidated by them. I felt as if we were being monitored all the time and that if we did or said anything out of turn, we would be singled out and asked to leave the training course. I struggled to pay attention in class and didn't see the purpose or value in a lot of what we were being taught. My worries were compounded by one of my trainers, who saw my struggles and tried to talk me into leaving the force at the first hurdle, advising me that I was young and that there would be a hard struggle ahead. I resisted the impulse to give up knowing that I was pursuing my childhood dream and that this was just "cold feet" and maybe a fear of the unknown.

There was one trainer who made this and other two week periods at HQ bearable as he was just so funny. There was a rumour that he had been sent to the training department due to being a bit of a liability as an officer on the street. He told us himself that whilst working at a busy city centre police station he had arrested a man for begging. Instead of taking the beggar to the police custody centre for the detention to be authorised and for an investigation to take place, he had taken him straight to the Magistrates Court. He demanded a hearing immediately and when he was told that the Magistrates had a schedule of cases to deal with and couldn't possibly fit in someone who hadn't even been through police custody, he read to them from the statute book covering police powers. He confidently quoted the statute which states that anyone arrested by a police officer for begging should be presented at a Magistrates Court within twenty-four hours of their arrest, and that this is what he was doing. Only a police officer can really understand how procedurally crazy his actions were.

On another occasion an off duty officer was sitting in traffic on his way home from work when he saw this same officer on duty in uniform walking across a pedestrian crossing in front of him. The officer suddenly stopped in the middle of the crossing to do an "Elvis pose" for a few seconds and then carried on walking as if nothing had happened! I could see why it had been necessary to move him somewhere less conspicuous than patrolling the streets, but was a little concerned that his position in the training department might lead to him passing on unusual ideas to us as new recruits. Over time I decided that "training" was probably the best place for him.

He was actually a really nice guy and brightened up my training experience. I could see that he really cared about us as individual recruits and was trying to ease our entry into a disciplined service. One of the most amusing things was that his fellow trainer was very "by the book"; they were like chalk and cheese but were forced to work together. It was obvious that each didn't like the other's methods, although they didn't admit this. They were both, therefore, constantly doing things to undermine each other during class, which we found highly entertaining. Neither was vicious or vindictive so it became a polite battle for control.

# CHAPTER FOUR

# Ashford Residential Training Centre, Kent

After the first two weeks at HQ it was time for residential training at Ashford in Kent (a one and a half hour drive from Sussex). Forces from across the local area sent their officers to Ashford, so I met officers from many other forces. It seemed as if the buildings had been there since time began and certainly many of the required customs and traditions had. I wondered if I had mistakenly joined the army rather than the police force.

We had our own small rooms and could go off site if we wanted but there was a curfew. Training school was mostly classroom based with written multiple choice exams every so often. I couldn't believe this: I had dropped out of university to get away from studying and yet here I was studying again. My teachers were once again frustrated as they knew I could do better in the exams if I studied harder, but I just wanted to pass and didn't see the point in doing extra work for a higher score. One of my friends took me to one side for a "serious talk" and told me that if I didn't get my head down and study properly, I would be sacked!

There were some unnecessarily bureaucratic rules in relation to the exam papers, though. For example, we were not allowed to compare our question and answer paper after the test to see which we had got wrong. I have no idea why this rule was in place as students really needed to know the correct answers when putting our training into practice on the street. On one test I memorised the positions of many of the questions and answers. On receiving my marks I knew that one of the answers that had been marked wrong was actually right (due to having studied Law at college). I queried this, which resulted in a bit of a scandal as "no one had done this before". Eventually the teachers admitted a mistake and changed my mark.

Maybe I went one step too far by asking if they were going to change the marks of all of the other students who had also taken the test. They definitely didn't appreciate it when I followed this up by casting doubt on the accuracy of the marking of the other questions on the test. How could I be sure they had been marked correctly when I was not allowed to check them? The spirit of cooperation vanished when I started down this road but the teachers thanked me for raising the initial concern and hastily moved on. Looking back I don't envy those teachers at all as I must have been a nightmare to manage.

At least the subject matter for the classroom work was interesting and it was possible that the things we were learning might become useful to us someday. There still seemed to be an element of detachment from reality and I found myself thinking during practical exercises that the scenarios would never occur in the real world. There was even a made-up town called Sandford where all of our fake scenarios took place.

Every day we were meant to spend hours shining our boots and preparing our uniform for parade. Eventually, most of the girls found male colleagues who had previously been in the army to help them with this tedious chore. It seemed that we could spend forever working on them without making any real difference otherwise. I still don't know what the purpose of all of this was, other than to admire each other's handiwork, as we never went outside the training school. Our boots and their comparative shininess did occupy a large chunk of our daily conversation as there wasn't much else to talk about.

The fire alarms sometimes went off in the middle of the night and we were expected to appear in formations on the parade ground within a matter of minutes. One night there was obviously a problem with the alarm which went off three times in the space of a few hours. This resulted in one young guy, obviously having had enough, appearing for parade in just a pair of boxer shorts and a duvet and lining up with the rest of us as we tried to choke back giggles. He was given short shrift and was later "required to resign" for a long string of misdemeanours. Honestly, I was surprised the force took as long as they did to deal with him as he was constantly in trouble from the outset. I did feel sorry for him, though, as he was likeable, but clearly training for the wrong job.

One really ineffective procedure was that every morning somebody, probably a staff member, called over the paging system either "ties on" or "ties off". This obviously meant that we should either wear our ties or not depending on the instruction, which was usually determined by the weather. The problem was that the paging system was muffled and due to the words being similar, no one could tell whether they had said "on" or "off". So for an hour or so after the instruction was given students rushed around asking other students, who also didn't know, for clarification of the dress for the day. This may not seem like a big deal, but if we happened to get it wrong and left the accommodation block without a tie on a "tie day", we were guaranteed not to get more than a few paces outside before a window from the staff accommodation block opposite would fly open and a "Where's your tie?" would be yelled at us, sending us scurrying back to the block for it.

We also had to acknowledge the staff members whenever we passed them in the grounds by saying, "Staff," in a clipped and formal tone, which felt like it needed to be followed by a salute, but fortunately this was not required. In my opinion, it was all a bit unnecessary and part of a bygone era, but most of the staff at the centre hadn't been on active duty for decades so it was easy to see why this had happened. In my view, employing these staff didn't make much sense from a training perspective as they often talked about situations that didn't exist outside the centre and hadn't done so for quite some time.

It was at training school that I developed a gambling problem. I had always had a propensity for this type of thing, being unable to resist the allure of the slot machines as a young child. As a teenager, unfortunately, there had been times when I had managed to double my money, much to the astonishment of my mother, who believed that gambling never pays. Generally in those days I was quite sensible and purchased some item of clothing with the extra money, but over time, more often than not, I would re-invest it in another machine and lose the lot.

There was a single machine at the training school with a maximum jackpot of £100. I spent many evenings playing the machine now that I was earning good money and hit the jackpot a few times during my four months but didn't make any money overall. It was one way to relieve the boredom of the evenings at training school as others drank beer and socialised at the bar. I was steering clear of alcohol in a desperate attempt to lose weight and work on my fitness as previously instructed. I lost two and a half stone in my four months at training school and had to make a special appearance at the clothing store to have all of my uniform refitted as I was now two sizes smaller. The woman at the clothing store, who always seemed severe and never spoke to anyone, broke her silence to say to me, "Just tell me one thing, how on earth did you do it?"

The consequence of my fitness training was that I developed really painful knees, I think as a repetitive strain injury from running and twisting on the wooden floor when turning for the bleep test. They grew so painful that I couldn't walk for days on end and had to sit out some of the physical training. I therefore failed the bleep test and was informed that I would get another chance to complete it back at Lewes HQ. If I failed a second time, I would be kicked out of the force. Now you can see why I started having nightmares about those bleeps.

One thing I will never forget and which could definitely be considered as "cruel and unusual punishment" was the compulsory Public Order Training that took place once a week. We were kitted out with shields and other heavy protective kit and then ran around the grounds after our trainer in single file, often in extreme heat. At times I was nearly crying from the exhaustion; others did cry but were largely ignored. The Public Order Training staff, who I am convinced were slightly mad, made us shield ourselves as bricks were thrown at us. We also took part in fire simulations. I really hated all of this stuff as I had joined the police to be an investigator, not to take part in this type of thing. Looking back, I would like to be able to say that it was worth it and useful later on, but in reality those who wanted to take part in this type of incident volunteered for it and were specially trained. The force recognised that not everyone was cut out for policing public order incidents. I was definitely afraid of the Public Order Trainers as they went through their crazy and dangerous routines week by week. It's a miracle no one was seriously hurt.

A parade officially took place at least once a week, but we practised marching in our assigned formations most lunchtimes because the former army personnel among us took it far too seriously. Apparently it was meant to teach us discipline, but I considered it pointless and couldn't see how it would be useful on the street. During the subsequent ten years I never had occasion to march anywhere after finishing training school, but I guess it made us look orderly and official whilst we were there. The tiresome practice was for a special Parade day at the end of our four months when our parents and friends were invited to see us "Pass Out" (or, complete our training). We paraded around to music, marching and saluting and then stood for several hours in the boiling heat whilst some speeches were given.

My parents came to watch on this grand occasion but I wasn't feeling very well. I was afraid to move as I stood rigidly in formation with my arms behind my back. I then choked repeatedly on nothing and felt tears running down my face as the fellow officers either side of me tried to establish, without causing a disturbance and drawing attention to themselves, whether I was okay. Others were not quite so lucky and literally passed out from the heat, slumping into various positions in front of their friends and family. It was a bit of a charade and, as it turned out, was what all former Ashford residents remembered as they proudly compared the lengths of time they had been forced to stand in formation. I was glad when that day and the four months of training were over!

Ashford Residential Training Centre has now been closed and replaced by the more modern method that requires attendance at university. I am pleased that no other poor souls will be forced to endure what I went through, although for balance I should add that not everyone found the experience unpleasant.

# CHAPTER FIVE

# Hove, Actually

We were asked for station preferences for our first permanent post and as I lived and had previously worked in the Worthing area, I asked if I could begin at Hove. I made it clear that under no circumstances would I be happy to be transferred to the neighbouring area of Brighton as I didn't like it. I found it claustrophobic and dark. I don't know why I felt like this as I hadn't been there more than a few times; I just remembered that when I had visited, everything felt very close together. Maybe it was just because I wasn't used to being in a city because I also felt like that in London. In the end, I was really pleased to be assigned to Hove as per my request.

Hove residents will understand the title of this chapter. Brighton is a better known, bigger place so people frequently asked the residents of Hove if they came from Brighton. The response from the more well-to-do persons was, "Hove, actually," as if they couldn't wait to make the distinction. There was even an occasion when I was on holiday in Spain talking to an ex-pat. I said I lived "near Brighton" and to my astonishment he responded, "Hove, actually."

My initial shift pattern in the force was one of two earlies (7am-4pm), two lates (3pm-12pm), and two nights (11pm-7am) with four days off at the end. The trick was to make sure that you got up at a reasonable time after sleeping in the day from the last night shift and then you could enjoy the rest of the days off. I never quite mastered it, though, and often slept all through my days off. Once I slept for thirty-six hours straight after a set of shifts and woke up thinking it was Sunday when it was Monday! I never adjusted properly to shift work and often struggled due to my body clock being out of sync, but this shift pattern was popular with the experienced staff and also considered to be best health-wise due to the regular routine.

To begin with I was being "tutored" by a more senior officer, which meant that we went to all of the incidents together. We were the first emergency response to 999 calls and other incidents, and mostly drove around in police cars looking for evidence of criminal activity. There were several "newbies", a term for the newest probationary officers working at Hove, and there was healthy competition between us. However, the pressure to perform was intense and sometimes caused officers to panic and take things too far. One officer was proven to have fabricated a story, saying that he had witnessed a crime taking place whilst he was out on patrol. A large amount of resources had been dedicated to locating the fictitious suspect and the officer was required to leave the force for dishonesty.

One of the first incidents I attended was a domestic dispute. On entering the premises I was confronted by an extremely skinny, hysterical lady with wide, fearful eyes, who grabbed me in a bear hug, shaking and crying. She was pointing to a large man sitting in the next room on a sofa with his back to us. I saw what looked like drug paraphernalia on the table and smashed pieces of pot plants and other furniture strewn around. I tried to comfort the lady and find out what had happened whilst my tutor spoke to the man. This was a difficult task for me; I was in total shock as I was just nineteen and had lived a pretty sheltered life. Here I was in the midst of a scene involving drugs and domestic abuse, two things I had never encountered before, and I was expected to make decisions about what happened next! We decided to escort the man from the premises. Afterwards, my tutor advised me that I shouldn't have allowed the woman to hang onto me and that I needed to make sure I kept my distance to retain authority in this type of situation. I humbly accepted the advice, wondering what I had got myself into.

The next domestic incident I attended was similarly shocking, when a twenty year old man answered the door to us stark naked. He then walked calmly around the flat relaying what had happened, making no attempt to cover his dignity, as if this was a perfectly normal way to behave. Whilst this was going on, the aggrieved woman in the next room, about twenty years his senior, yelled and screamed insults at him and every so often attempted to enter the room and attack him. Needless to say we didn't allow the woman to attack the man and we made him put some clothes on before arresting him.

Another case during my early days at Hove that stayed with me is that of a well-known soul singer. I was very interested in pop music as a teenager and listened to it avidly, and so was well aware of the band that this singer fronted. You can imagine my shock, therefore, when I turned up at an address to investigate a shoplifting charge and the singer answered the door. Sadly, her life had gone steadily downhill since the days when the band had been very popular. Evidence of her celebrity lifestyle was still visible on the racks of fashionable clothes in her basement flat. I couldn't understand how someone's circumstances could change so drastically over the course of a few years and was stunned at the path her life had taken simply because of the decisions she had made. Shortly after that, tragedy struck as the singer fled the scene of another shoplifting and was run over by several vehicles, killing her immediately, and reminding me of the brevity of life.

I was quickly introduced to the local criminal youths, who had a total lack of respect for authority. They were responsible for most of the low level petty crime in the area although sometimes they graduated to more serious crime like vehicle theft. One night we drove around a corner whilst on routine patrol to find a smart car on its roof in the middle of the road. The trade plates were the only obvious identification marks for the vehicle and there was a lone baseball cap in the back. We knew we would be able to obtain forensic evidence to identify the culprits later, but what amazed me was how these teenagers seemed to have nine lives. I would have expected at least one of them to have been seriously injured in a crash like that, but they had got out completely unscathed and run off, probably to do it again. We drove around for a while seeking the original location of the vehicle and eventually found a car showroom minus one car and with a slight gap where the doors had been forced open.

Generally these kids would get a "slap on the wrist" if they did make it to court, not really teaching them the lessons they needed to learn. It is a shocking indictment of our legal system that most of these same boys are now in prison serving long sentences for crimes including robbery, burglary, grievous bodily harm, and in one tragic case murder; the victim was one of the boys from the original group. I was thankful not to have been on duty when this happened, having swapped my shift with a colleague, otherwise I would have been supervising the terrible murder scene. For those who think the police are heavy handed and don't care about the people they are dealing with, some officers were walking around in tears for weeks after the murder took place; they just couldn't believe that this had happened to one of the boys whom they dealt with regularly. I remember these kids when they were just eleven and twelve writing graffiti tags and receiving public order warnings for swearing.

By far the most unbelievable incident we were called to when I was stationed at Hove was to six-year-olds damaging cars. I still remember the controller giving us details of the incident over the radio as my crew mate and I sat in stunned silence while the age registered. But sure enough, on arrival at the scene there were several *very* small children dashing around amongst parked vehicles and some angry parents exchanging words out in the street. Needless to say we didn't make any arrests on that occasion.

I also recall whilst on patrol one late evening seeing a group of young boys boldly marching along the main road in a line, proudly carrying various articles of street furniture including a large road cone and a very long sign board on their shoulders. Children often "borrowed" such items and hid them elsewhere or took them home for a while as souvenirs, but this time they had been caught red-handed. The look of shock on their faces, as we pulled our police vehicle up alongside them and gave them five minutes to return the items to their original positions, was priceless. In these situations it was necessary to wait until the kids had soberly left to do as we instructed before laughing. We liked the children with character that made our work entertaining at times, and we wondered what crazy ideas they would come up with next.

I realised over time that there were just a handful of people committing most of the crime as we were dealing with the same offenders time and time again. The domestic incidents were also at the same addresses every week and the systems that were in place didn't seem to be achieving much in many cases. Ultimately, we couldn't force a victim of domestic violence to report it to us or to leave the perpetrator, although our powers did increase if there were children involved. Years later the law changed to allow "victimless" prosecutions, where we could use any evidence of assault to prosecute the offender even against the wishes of the victim. The attitude of the courts also changed to allow prosecutions where it was one person's word against the other with no independent witnesses, as was often the case in domestic violence incidents. Before these measures were put in place we felt powerless and often went through the motions of arresting the perpetrator as required by policy, but with little hope of a positive outcome.

# CHAPTER SIX

# Dealing with Death

My first suicide case had a profound effect on me and taught me that individual officers each respond differently to trauma. We had received a report of a missing person, a middle aged lady who had been feeling depressed. Her family were very worried as she had left a note for them stating her suicidal intent, but as this wasn't the first time, they weren't sure how to react. Our supervisory officers decided this was an urgent matter and allocated all of the officers on duty to search for the woman. We spent hours traipsing through the town covering all of the ground and ended up on the beach. Sadly, after some time an officer called on the radio to say he had found the woman's body. Honestly, at that moment I was just glad it hadn't been me who had made the discovery as I dreaded the thought of being alone with a dead body. We went to the location and stood around the deceased lady. I was in a state of shock as I had never seen a dead body before. I felt awkward but incredibly sad for the poor woman and her family.

A senior officer told me that as the trainee I would need to check and search the body; I was to search for any obvious injuries, medication or anything of value that might need to be seized by the police to prevent theft or as part of the investigation into her death. I felt really uncomfortable with this, especially as all the other officers were gathered around and I was still processing my emotions regarding the death of the lady. As I bent down to start the search, the senior officer present shone a torch on her face saying loudly, "She blinked," causing me to jump back in shock. Some of the other officers laughed as I started shaking. I told them it wasn't funny but realised later that this type of humour is a defence mechanism used by some officers to process emotions associated with trauma, but to me at the time it seemed totally inappropriate. This was my first experience of death at the age of just nineteen.

My second experience was a more standard call relating to an older lady who had died in the night, but it was no easier for me to deal with. In fact, I always found dealing with dead bodies difficult no matter what the circumstances were. On this occasion I was left upstairs with the woman, who was lying on the floor next to her bed. I was checking the room whilst my colleague was downstairs talking to the large number of relatives who had gathered. As I searched the room, I came across a bin that was full of blood and other bodily fluids. I wasn't expecting this, so I panicked and a sudden desperation to be away from the dead person and to be back in the company of living people hit me. I hurried to get out of the room but tripped over the body as I did so and ended up hyperventilating at the top of the staircase, leaning on the banister as I tried to calm down. My colleague came upstairs and when I told him what had happened, he took control of the situation, advising me that I must get a grip of myself as the relatives were downstairs. We realised later that the lady had haemorrhaged and that it had been a natural death with no suspicious circumstances, which helped me to process my emotions.

I tended to get too emotionally involved with individuals at times, wanting to help people even when it was impossible. I responded to a report of a suicidal man at his home address one day. His ex-girlfriend had made the call as she was worried about some of the things he had been saying to her. I arrived at a tiny bedsit property which was just large enough to hold a bed. The man was in bed in his nightwear in the middle of the day looking thoroughly dejected, totally without hope. One thing that stood out was a bowl lying on the bed that was completely filled with what must have been over one hundred cigarette ends. I wondered how long it had taken him to accumulate these; maybe just a few days.

After checking the man's welfare and confirming verbally that he wasn't planning to harm himself, we had to leave as there was nothing we could do for him. Our powers were limited in this area. While we could call a doctor to consider sectioning him to a mental health hospital for his own protection, in practice the doctors were rarely willing to attend and often released people whom we considered a risk to themselves straight back into the community after a cursory assessment. If we had been really worried about an imminent danger to the man, our best option would have been somehow to lure him outside and then arrest him using police powers under the Mental Health Act for his own protection; he would then have to be assessed by a doctor in police custody. This may seem somewhat unethical, but as this law could only be enforced in a public place and protecting someone's life is a priority, it was sometimes what we did.

# CHAPTER SEVEN

# Urgent Assistance

Throughout my police service there were three things that caused everyone to drop everything that they were doing and go rushing en masse out of the station. If we heard, on the police radio, the words "intruders on", "runners" or "10/20", nothing else mattered apart from reaching the location of the officer who had uttered the words as quickly as possible. "Intruders on" meant that an officer had inadvertently or otherwise found suspected burglars in the process of committing a burglary; they were still "on" the premises. This was a rarity of course, hence the urgency. The idea here was to get as many people as possible there to shut down the area and prevent the suspect making an escape by gradually closing in on them. Everybody wanted to catch a burglar in the act as they would become the station "hero" for a short time, until something better came along, that is.

"Runners" was as simple as it sounds; it meant that people were running. This may seem curious at first but usually the circumstances were such that the officer believed that the people were running having committed some sort of crime and that they required assistance to catch the "runners". Having said that, there were several occasions where the officers were mistaken and, after a long and intensive search involving many resources and sometimes a helicopter, the "runners" were eventually captured only to state that they were only running because the police were chasing them and they didn't know why! This was a particular problem with foreign students, who ran particularly quickly, because they had sometimes originated in countries where, if they were being chased by the police and were subsequently captured, they might be robbed, beaten or killed.

"10/20" used to be the police code for "urgent assistance" which normally meant that an officer was in serious trouble. It has now been replaced by an emergency button attached to the police radios but officers still use the verbal code sometimes as it wakes everyone up. On hearing the code or anything like it, officers who sometimes hadn't been seen for weeks or even months working in undercover or specialist departments would emerge from all over the station to join the throng. Numerous cars would go screeching at top speed out of the station, sirens wailing and lights flashing. Sometimes, this happened before there was a location given, until one CCTV operator pointed out that he could see all of the police vehicles criss-crossing all over the town at high-speed like Pacman. This was obviously dangerous to civilians and other vehicles so it was ingrained in us that we must wait for a location before we sped off anywhere. While this makes sense, it was extremely hard in practice, knowing a colleague was in trouble somewhere.

In the Hove days most of the "10/20" shouts tended to come from Brighton officers as Brighton was a busier and more dangerous place to work. If we were able to respond to those incidents to help out the Brighton officers, we would, but I was always glad to return to Hove after seeing the kind of craziness going on in Brighton and the dangerous situations that officers were facing on a daily basis. I attended one such incident with a senior officer who completely lost his temper with me as he was driving at high speeds through the back alleys of Brighton and I was unsuccessfully navigating whilst being thrown around in the vehicle. I've never been that successful at navigating anything.

We had a lot of fun during quiet periods, especially on night shifts whilst driving around on patrol. (I'm not going to ruin the fun of current officers by giving details here.) Some of the games had to stop when GPS was fitted, as supervisors and CCTV operators would no doubt have had some questions if they had seen the patterns of activity. There was also a fake cycling proficiency test that new officers were forced to perform in the backyard at Hove station whilst all the regular officers crowded round an upstairs window to watch and laugh. These were traditions passed down from previous generations of officers and helped to lighten the burdens of some of the things we were dealing with.

# CHAPTER EIGHT

# Early Mistakes

Obtaining independent patrol is a milestone in the life of any new police officer. It means that after ten weeks they are finally allowed to go it alone, to head out onto the streets and make decisions without someone watching their every move. It is also an intimidating experience as suddenly the officer is alone on the street and if there is any type of incident, the public look immediately to them as a uniformed authority figure regardless of age or life experience. That individual is now "The Police" and they are there to serve and protect.

At Hove, I reached independent patrol after fifteen weeks; a slow learner, I guess. I found a great sense of freedom in being out on the street alone but I also quickly realised that the vast majority of people's concerns were trivial. I was asked to give directions, investigate arguments about threats on social media or by text message, normally beginning with "My boyfriend's best friend's sister" or similar, and to mediate in disputes between the local groups of drunks who congregated in the area.

I built relationships with the local people in the community and regularly patrolled the crime "hot spots" identified by patterns of criminal activity. I was interested in people as individuals and enjoyed obtaining information and intelligence from people I met. I was inquisitive by nature which helped in this respect and I had a good eye for things that "weren't quite right". I stopped a teenager on one occasion because he seemed to be high on some type of substance and, sure enough, I found that he had many aerosol cans in his rucksack. I had no real idea about solvent abuse, although I was aware that it existed. Some colleagues came to assist me and the boy agreed to allow us to dispose of the cans. The law didn't really allow us to do much as the substances weren't illegal and he wasn't committing any crime so we had to let him go. Sadly, over time this boy's habit grew and even though his family intervened to send him to rehab, he died in his twenties.

Over the years, this was one of the hardest things for me to accept as many of the names and faces that I recalled from past misdemeanours disappeared from police records having died as a result of drug overdoses, suicide or, more rarely, murder. But they stayed with me; it never became normal for me as I saw each individual as a life that had chosen the wrong path and I felt desperately sorry for them. I was saddened that some officers seemed happy when a prolific burglar supporting a drug habit died from a heroin overdose having just been released from prison. Of course, not all officers adopted this attitude but the culture at that time was very much that it was one less burglar to worry about.

On another occasion I made a mistake which I was fortunately given the opportunity to rectify. Whenever an officer arrests a person on a warrant that has been issued by a court or other authority, it is that officer's responsibility to cancel the circulation on the Police National Computer (PNC) so that they don't get arrested again for the same matter. The PNC is a database used across the country by all of the police forces. It holds basic data about individuals who have been arrested by the police at some point in their lives. It contains the details if they are wanted for any crime and gives intelligence about diseases they may have or weapons they may carry as well as other information. It is used regularly by police officers.

A few months earlier, I had stopped and arrested a man in the street in Hove who was wanted in a different force area for a relatively minor crime. He said that he was being threatened in that area, which was the reason for his appearance in Sussex. Actually, all this guy needed to do if he was really being threatened in the other part of the country was move away to a new area (as he had done) and then blend in with the community (which he hadn't). Unless his warrant was for a serious crime, all he had to do was act and behave like a normal member of society and no one would ever know there was a warrant for his arrest. As it was, my attention was drawn to him because of his behaviour. I never understood why wanted criminals didn't make more of an effort to blend in as the chances of us finding them would be slim, but they always seemed to do things that made them stand out like a sore thumb.

On this day I saw him again and because I recognised him due to the previous arrest, I approached him and checked him on the PNC. To my surprise there was still a "wanted" marker under his details. As the radio traffic can be heard by many officers, my supervisor started arranging to send backup when he heard the status of the man as he knew I was alone. However, the guy kept telling me that the matter had already been dealt with and when I checked the specific details, I discovered that it was the previous warrant that I had already arrested him for. I must have forgotten to cancel it. It took a while to convince my supervisor that the matter had been dealt with. I was just grateful that it had been me who had stopped him again as any other officer would surely have arrested him and then there may have been a case of unlawful arrest to deal with.

Another area that was frequently subject to mistakes was the searching of prisoners. We were taught to search our vehicles both before and after a prisoner was placed in the back of them but in practice this didn't always happen due to a combination of busyness and, if I'm honest, complacency. It was one of those things that tended only to become routine once you had personally faced a dangerous situation as a result of a failure to search properly. Colleagues found large kitchen knives, drugs and various other implements under the back seats of vehicles.

On arresting a prisoner, we would take them straight to Brighton custody. This was before the large purpose built centre at Hollingbury and at a time when the custody sergeants were highly feared, especially amongst probationary officers. They tended to ask difficult questions of the newer staff, probably to ensure they knew the procedures for the future. Once you had been an officer for a few years and your name became known, it was a lot easier.

On one occasion I arrested a man for shoplifting. I hadn't carried out a full search of the male prisoner on arriving at the custody centre as the normal procedure at the time was to search them after their detention had been authorised. Sometimes if the cell block was busy, it was necessary to wait in a holding cell on arriving at custody. My prisoner decided he needed to use the toilet whilst we were waiting so after trying in vain to find a male officer willing to escort him, I asked permission to take him myself and then did so. I kept the door open as he sat on the toilet but obviously I felt uncomfortable and tried to appear as if I was looking away whilst maintaining a minimum level of observation. Then he began grunting and groaning and making all sorts of noises which made me even more uncomfortable.

After quite some time another officer and I entered the toilet cell to check his progress and discovered to our horror that the toilet bowl was empty and that he had somehow managed to inject himself with drugs using a syringe that had been secreted somewhere on his person. Then everything went crazy as an alarm was pressed and half a dozen custody sergeants rushed in to take control of the situation. I'm not sure what happened from that point on but I remember seeing the words "jacked up in cell" on the whiteboard space next to his name and for several weeks afterwards the custody sergeants gave me severe looks and mentioned the matter whenever I brought prisoners in.

Sometime later I was forced to strip search a female prisoner who was a known drug user. Strip searching is something that most officers detest although many of the prisoners seem to think differently, commenting that we must be enjoying ourselves as they endure the humiliation of having to remove their clothes in front of us. This woman had a note on her record suggesting that she had previously secreted drugs in a certain area of her back where she had a wound from an injury. Clearly it was necessary to search this area, which was covered over with a temporary bandage, but when I attempted to do this, she started shouting about the indignity of it all. Normal practice is to ask the prisoner themselves to search the area by demonstrating that there is nothing there, for example, by pulling out the pocket lining in trousers. This woman refused and accused me of humiliating her by suggesting that she might keep drugs inside this area of her body; the fact that she had previously done this failed to register on her horizon.

Despite the previous record, I felt terrible at having to make the request as I felt sorry for her; she was a long-term drug addict and her body really was a mess. I searched the area as best as I could and mentioned to the sergeant what had happened. It turned out that she did manage to keep a tablet or two on her person as she was later taken to hospital suspected of having consumed drugs. Whether they were in the area I had searched, I don't know, but this demonstrates the difficulties we had when searching people and how it's not always as straightforward as outsiders might think, especially when trying to balance a person's human right to dignity with the possibility of them harming themselves or others.

One day I had cause to arrest an eighty-seven-year-old man on suspicion of criminal damage and section five of the Public Order Act (causing harassment, alarm or distress). The latter has now been adapted to be used in all manner of circumstances that I'm sure were not in mind when the government brought in the legislation. In those days it was used sporadically and, in my opinion, more effectively. The adapted Public Order Act is now a bit like Anti-Social-Behavioural-Orders, which started out as a good idea to limit the freedoms and behaviour of a small minority of not-so-good citizens, but became a sought after label of status for the next generation of youth. I remember a time when our local misguided youths were collecting police stop search forms and judging each other's street credibility on this alone. Clearly, in today's society (at least amongst some youth) the more times you have been stopped by the police the better friend or associate you make.

Anyway, back to the old man I was compelled to present at Brighton custody as there didn't seem a viable alternative. I realised that there might be a problem immediately as the custody sergeant looked shocked when he shuffled to stand in front of her desk and even more concerned when he mumbled a long list of medical issues in response to her questions. To be honest, I didn't know that there was an option to deal with people outside custody in these types of cases as voluntary interviews were not in common use. As far as I was aware anyone over the age of ten was arrested and taken to custody, end of story. I did feel a bit awkward as he reminded me of someone's granddad. The sergeant obviously also felt uncomfortable as she addressed the man very respectfully as "Sir" and set about ensuring that he didn't keel over during his stay. I don't think anything came of the original "crime" in the end but I certainly learnt my lesson; don't arrest anyone who might suffer from incontinence or who might not survive the experience and don't try to present them at custody at Brighton.

# CHAPTER NINE

# Giving Evidence in Court

The first appearance as a witness in court is something that every new officer fears. Magistrates Court can be worse than Crown Court as, to put it bluntly, Magistrates are volunteers with no compulsory legal training and therefore at times they misunderstand the culture and practices of the police force. Sometimes they made decisions demonstrating that they felt excessively sorry for the offender(s) and were more easily taken in by them. Later in my service, during an appearance at Worthing Magistrates Court, the Magistrates believed a male suspect's evidence, despite his previous convictions and the five police officers that gave evidence to the contrary.

My first case involved a drink driver I had arrested a few months previously. It was the first case I had been involved in where a suspect had pleaded not guilty, making my attendance required at court. I had found the man sleeping at the wheel of his vehicle on what later turned out to be private property at the edge of a public road. He was drunk, as confirmed by the failed breath test I had administered. I arrested him on suspicion of being drunk in charge of a motor vehicle and cautioned him. Under caution he made various comments to me including that he had driven to the location after drinking. I wrote my statement shortly after the incident and the man was later charged.

The police caution is one of those anomalies in life that I have never really understood. It reads, "You do not have to say anything, but it may harm your defence if you do not mention, when questioned, something which you later rely on in court. Anything you do say can be given in evidence." A relatively intelligent person with some knowledge of legal procedures may be able to understand this lengthy instruction if they really think about it. By law we were forced to spout this entire statement every time we arrested someone and I can virtually guarantee that 95% of the people being arrested had no idea what we were talking about. Most of them were drunk or enraged having committed violent crime, or high on drugs or angry and upset at being arrested. There was no way they had the mental capacity at that time seriously to consider the meaning and consequences of the police caution. I feel it's one of many legal processes documented by someone who doesn't have much familiarity with the practicalities of policing.

I once heard a colleague tell a prisoner, "I'm arresting you on suspicion of being drunk and disorderly... you do not have to say anything *blah, blah, blah,*" because the prisoner was drunk, obnoxious, aggressive and not listening at all to the caution. I laughed on hearing this because this particular colleague was usually fairly straight-laced but I guess he knew it didn't really matter; the caution wasn't that relevant because there wasn't anything the prisoner could have said in mitigation. He was drunk and disorderly, case closed.

In relation to the drink driver, what I should have done is stuck rigidly to my original statement of events written soon after the incident, but as I was being questioned by various lawyers, I started trying to think back to what had actually been said in an effort to be extra truthful and to give the court the full facts. This definitely backfired as when there was a slight conflict between what I was saying in court and the version of events I had written in my witness statement, the Magistrates asked me whether my memory of events in court was better than it had been on the day I wrote the statement all those months ago. I didn't know how to answer this and got myself tied up in knots. In the end, after forty-five minutes of gruelling questioning, the case was thrown out and I returned to my station with my tail between my legs. Needless to say, after that I always stuck to my statement of events, regardless of later considerations, and my court experiences became a lot more pleasant.

I wish I could say the same for one of my police officer colleagues, who returned from court one day having given evidence and having been accused of deliberately misleading the court by the judge, an extremely serious accusation. Matters went from bad to worse when the judge later wrote a letter to our sergeant outlining his complaints about this officer. I happened upon them as our sergeant was unsuccessfully attempting to impress upon the officer the serious nature of the complaint, exacerbated of course by the fact that it had come from a judge. Knowing this officer, who probably fell foul of the judge due to cheekiness or some other such harmlessness in any normal environment, I was not surprised when, on returning from giving evidence in court and in front of a different judge on the next occasion, and being asked how it had gone, my colleague quickly and effortlessly quipped, "Letter's in the post, Sarge," with a grin.

# CHAPTER TEN

# Training World

During an officer's initial two year probationary period, time is allotted for additional two week training courses back at Sussex Police Headquarters, Lewes. I dreaded these courses as, when I managed to attend the lessons on time (not helped by the ridiculous on-site parking situation), I often found myself in trouble for not properly engaging in the lessons or for expressing contrary opinions. I even recall on one occasion being given an after-class lesson by a trainer (who took his job a tad too seriously) in how to sit properly on my chair to prove that I was paying attention. The fact that the trainers should also carry some level of responsibility for keeping the attention of the students by making the lessons relevant and interesting didn't always seem to be a consideration. Having said that, there were some exceptions and some interesting classes and trainers.

The parking situation at Lewes is worthy of further comment as it was the bane of every officer's life. Officers and students who were not usually working at HQ (me) were only allowed to park in dedicated areas which filled up quickly as there were many more people than spaces. The bottom car park was in a sort of field with overgrown grass and bushes extending into the parking area; it was called the "Dog Field". Drivers parked wherever they could, often at obscure and difficult angles or squashed into virtually impossible spaces leaving little manoeuvring space. Sometimes cars would be hanging over the edge of the ditches at the bottom of the field, the drivers caring little for the problems caused for other vehicles, which resulted in everyone developing a similar attitude.

Having sat in the Lewes tunnel for thirty minutes, also a twice daily frustration, I arrived very late for class one day and having driven around the already full "Dog Field" to no avail, I proceeded to follow the example of several other drivers; I drove my car onto the patch of nice, green, freshly mowed grass outside the large building at the front of HQ. I later learnt this was the Resourcing Centre, where all the emergency calls were received, but at this time I had no clue. I just thought that the management had helpfully provided an extra parking area and as I wasn't the first or only driver to think this I didn't think any more about it. I parked, locked up and headed off to my first lesson, preparing to be told off for being late.

Later, on returning to my vehicle, I was surprised not only to find that it was the only one still parked on the grass but that there was also a note attached to my windscreen. The handwritten note advised me in no uncertain terms that not only was I wrong to have assumed that this was an extra parking area but that due to the audacity I had had to park there, I was now banned from parking anywhere on site and would instead have to pay to park in one of the residential neighbourhoods nearby. I was a bit upset by this decision which had been made with no consultation and without any consideration of my reasons for parking in such a "visibly public spot".

I knew from my limited experience of HQ that this type of decision would not easily be overturned or disputed now that it had been made. Regular officers referred to their two week stints at HQ as "Training world" or "Headquarters land" as they blatantly dismissed many of the things they had been taught there; this was reminiscent of similar comments made about the residential training school as "Planet Ashford". For balance, I should add that this view is not shared by everyone and that some of the training was probably useful to some officers, but I have always disliked training courses and often found them to be a waste of time.

Anyway, I decided to approach my classroom trainer about my parking ban due to the considerable inconvenience of having to park off-site. He was very helpful at first and agreed to look into the matter when I explained the circumstances. I started to get my hopes up that a resolution might be found. Sadly, it was not to be and the way the trainer dealt with the matter definitely made me wish that I hadn't asked for his "help" in the first place. He started by stating that he had been shown exactly where I had parked and asked me to go and look at the location with him. I responded that I knew where I had parked as it was me that had parked there and that therefore this action was unnecessary.

He then told me several stories, going into great detail, all of which involved the events leading up to his "character" in the story parking illegally. On concluding each of his stories, he asked me what I would expect to happen if I were the "character" in the story. I found myself repeatedly saying, "Yes, I know I parked in the wrong place and I'm sorry about that but I'm asking if the decision can be reversed," only then to be told another story with different circumstance and a different character to prove the same point: that I had parked incorrectly. By the end of the conversation, I wanted to go and bang my head against a brick wall somewhere. The management didn't overturn the ban in the end and it was later brought in for all officers attending training courses.

# CHAPTER ELEVEN

# Trainees to the Rescue

If there was ever a major incident within Sussex requiring a large number of extra officers, the first place Senior officers looked was the various training courses taking place at Headquarters as officers could easily be extracted from these with minimal disruption to normal policing operations. (Perhaps it also says something about the value they placed on the things we were being taught on these courses.) These emergency incidents always occurred at inconvenient times, usually on a Friday afternoon as we were just finishing for the week and looking forward to the weekend. Twice my course group were called upon to attend such incidents.

The first incident was the Potters Bar Rail Crash in Hertfordshire. After the initial groans at being informed that it was necessary for us to stay on duty for the foreseeable future, we became more cooperative as we heard the terrible details of the tragedy, and by the end of the briefing all of us would have done anything that we could to help with the situation. As it was, we were needed to man phone lines as part of a Casualty Bureau Hotline that was to be set up for relatives and friends of the people who were, or may have been, on the train that de-railed. I was very nervous as I was still relatively inexperienced in policing terms and didn't know if I was ready to deal with grieving relatives and friends, especially as I was not allowed to give out any information, only to take their details for a call back later. I needn't have worried as it turned out we only stayed for a couple of hours and

I personally received no calls. Sadly, seven people died and over seventy were injured in the crash.

The second tragic case required a much more lengthy involvement. It relates to the murder of school teacher Jane Longhurst in Brighton. My training class was again summoned from HQ on a Friday to assist the Major Crime Branch (MCB). MCB were a large team of detectives and senior officers who dealt with murder cases and sometimes other serious crime requiring a large team and ongoing investigation. Although they had a main base, they tended to move around according to where they were working, taking all of their resources with them. They were called in by the local Criminal Investigation Department (CID) automatically for certain types of incidents.

I became part of the house to house team for the missing person investigation with many other officers and was required to work long hours with few breaks for the first few days. We were basically visiting every house in every street near the home address of the lady to try to establish her whereabouts. The questionnaires caused some controversy as they were very personal and very detailed in places. Some people refused to allow us even to enter their houses whilst others became incensed by some of the questions. The descriptive questions were the most bizarre, asking whether the person had visible nose hair or bushy eyebrows. We were initially told by our supervisors that we must ask all of the questions but after a few days they relented and allowed us to skip some of the more inflammatory questions as the tales of woe continued. These questionnaires had apparently proven to be effective in previous cases both in Sussex and elsewhere, the idea being that the details can be cross-checked to try to account for every person living/visiting in the area. I accepted the validity of the questionnaires but sometimes wondered if they would reveal anything that would give the investigation a proper lead.

On returning home one night I suddenly recalled a piece of information that I had received, not during the house to house enquiries but during my regular police work, and with a start I realised that the information could be crucial to the missing person investigation. I wished I had remembered the information before, but the more I thought about it, the more I knew I had to pass it up the chain to the lead investigators on the case. With trepidation I tried to call the incident room, wondering what on earth I would say and hoping that whoever answered the phone wouldn't make me feel stupid for having brought the information to their attention. I couldn't get through to the incident room.

The next day I went straight to the detectives leading the investigation and told them what I knew. To their credit they didn't say anything negative and the information was passed on. Later that day I was in a small room crammed full of about one hundred people, including very senior officers, with only a handful wearing uniform as most were detectives in plain clothes. We were waiting to be briefed on the planned action for the missing person investigation that day. I was mortified when I was suddenly called by name and asked to provide my information to the whole room of people. I was still just a young probationer with less than two years' police service and my ambition was to work within CID. That they considered my information of such importance that they wanted it directly from the source came as a surprise but I didn't want to look foolish in front of them so I managed somehow to stutter through a summary of what I knew. After the meeting, they put six detectives on the information as it was "the best lead they had had so far". In actual fact, the information was a total red herring that had nothing to do with the case in the end but at the time we didn't know that and it was important to check it out. Sadly weeks later Jane's body was found and a man was tried and convicted for her murder, not once, but twice after getting his conviction overturned on appeal.

Whilst working on this case I witnessed the painstaking detail that is required by detectives working on a missing person or murder investigation and how organised everything has to be from the outset. You can't just pursue leads at random as the detectives in TV series do. Everything has to be done in an orderly way and at a slow and deliberate pace to make sure nothing is missed. We, as the uniformed officers, were doing a lot of the slow and detailed work and I couldn't wait for the day that I was in CID and would be able to be part of the decision making processes and have access to all of the information about the investigation. Of course, a lot still depended on the supervisors leading the team as it was really down to them whether they shared the information or not and how they managed and led their team. But even so, I was still looking forward to reaching the dizzy heights of CID one day.

## CHAPTER TWELVE

# Did You Say Brighton?

Less than a year after I had joined the police, Hove and Shoreham division redefined their boundaries, merging Brighton with Hove and Shoreham with Worthing. I was to be posted to the new Brighton division and to be stationed at Central Brighton. I resisted this at first, reminding my supervisors that I had previously said I would work anywhere other than Brighton, but my protests fell on deaf ears. The force has a rule allowing them to transfer officers anywhere within a one hour drive or thirty miles of their home address and they regularly used this. I guess the term "posted" was quite appropriate in the way the management moved us at times; snap decisions and short notice periods prior to transfer made us feel as if we were envelopes rather than people!

In my case, though, the forcible transfer worked in my favour as I gained massive amounts of experience in a very short space of time. I enjoyed patrolling alone in the city and often made arrests as a result of stopping and checking people, especially the regular drunk people who congregated in certain areas. Officers often wrongly assumed their "wanted" status had already been checked. The easiest way for wanted people to go undetected was to hide in plain sight by becoming so familiar to local police that they made incorrect assumptions.

There was one area of Brighton that was considered off limits to lone patrolling officers, but I was only informed of this after I had been into it one day and found numerous discarded needles and blood all over the walls. It was an abandoned building at the bottom of North Road in which many of the local homeless people had taken up residence. There was an upstairs area up a narrow, twisting metal flight of stairs which looked as if it may become detached and fall to the floor if anyone tried to use it. Officers reported entering the building at night after hearing screaming and then nearly being hit by someone who came hurtling down the staircase and rushed out into the night without looking back. The state of the building made me dread to think what had gone on inside it in recent months. It was like looking into a different world, but even then I felt sad when I thought of those enslaved to alcohol and drug addictions, and wondered how they had ended up there. Many of them were pleasant to talk to and polite, lovable rogues, although there were some who had a vicious or nasty streak so it was necessary to be alert when dealing with them. Eventually the building was closed and sealed by the council due to becoming a health hazard, and the inhabitants moved to an even more dangerous location nearby.

On another day I was patrolling on foot alone in Brighton when the CCTV operator for the city centre advised all officers on the radio that a prolific drug user and thief was walking around in the centre. I knew the man and decided to look for him. After a brief search I saw his vehicle. It was parked illegally in an unusual location, partly on the pavement, in the middle of the city centre down the side of some shops. I guessed that the driver would return soon so I set about making arrangements for the vehicle to be recovered to the police pound. The vehicle was what the police call a "pool vehicle". Basically, it belongs to a criminal network but has no registered keeper and is often used in crime by any number of different people. Police powers allowed us to recover vehicles if we believed they would be used in crime, although sometimes we had to debate the decision with our seniors as it obviously cost money and could be hard to prove if there was a challenge by someone claiming to be the real owner.

However, I hadn't got very far in the procedure when the man appeared running towards me while I was standing by his vehicle. He looked shocked when he saw me and hesitated before continuing his progression at a slower pace. It wasn't really possible for him to turn around and make good his escape as he knew I had already seen him; he knew he would have to answer my questions. He was jiggling his legs around as I was talking to him, unable to stay still. I used my radio to contact someone at the nearby store from which he had just emerged, to ask if they had had any problems or had anything stolen. They radioed back stating that a woman's purse had been stolen from her handbag. A male colleague and I searched the man and, incredibly, we found the purse hidden up one of his trouser legs! No wonder he was fidgeting. I learnt to enjoy this type of success as it was a rare occurrence.

When a person is arrested they are taken to the nearest custody centre, where a custody sergeant decides whether their first period of twenty-four hour detention will be authorised for an investigation to take place. I arrested three young women for shoplifting and for stealing my cigarettes from my trouser pocket during the arrest and took them to custody. As they were being booked in by the custody sergeant, they were arguing with me about various things and then became physically aggressive as they were being searched and had to be restrained. The custody sergeant asked me with a touch of humour, "Natalie, why is it that whenever I am on duty you are always standing in front of this desk with female teenage prisoners and they are always kicking off?" I offered an innocent open-palmed gesture with a shoulder shrug as I answered, "I really don't know, Sarge."

Over time I learnt that most hunches or a sense that something isn't quite right are correct and should be explored. It can be tempting to brush it aside or convince yourself that you are imagining things, especially if it is necessary to draw colleagues into the investigation and potentially waste their time as well as your own, but most hunches prove justified. I dealt with an incident one day that made me even more certain of this. We had been given information about a suspicious address, where drug deals were likely taking place, to keep an eye on during our shifts. I drove to the location frequently hoping to see something or someone, and eventually it paid off. I saw two men hanging around outside the address so I stopped them and asked for their details. They gave their details confidently and were very cooperative so I didn't suspect anything. I checked the men on the Police National Computer and although they were both known to the police there was nothing outstanding for them and no active warrants, which confirmed what I was expecting based on their demeanour.

However, the PNC operator indicated that there were two possible records for one of them. The second record was under a different name with the same birth date and this man was an absconder from a local prison. I still thought it must just be a mistake and the man said that this mistake had been made previously with him being detained before, and that it should have been sorted out already. To be absolutely sure, I checked the description of the man I had stopped against both PNC records and found that he had parts of the descriptions of both records including a tattoo and a scar. Now I was totally confused as this was almost impossible. When the descriptions are recorded the person's DNA and fingerprints are also taken to make sure the correct description ends up with the correct person.

I had a tough call to make; should I believe him and let him go as he was very convincing, or arrest him to ascertain his true identity and risk being sued for unlawful arrest if he wasn't the other man and our systems were incorrect? I knew that if I didn't arrest him and check I would always wonder, so I risked wasting everyone's time, including my own, and took him to custody.

The custody sergeant was none too impressed when I tried to explain that I wanted to run a live check on the man's fingerprints to ascertain his identity but he authorised his detention for that purpose. Throughout the entire process this man was extremely pleasant and good-natured, assuring me and the sergeant that there had been a mistake, and we believed him. He repeated this several times even as he was having his fingerprints taken, and I was almost completely sure I had made a mistake and wasted everyone's time. I dreaded the result and looking foolish in front of everyone.

When the result came back, the staff member who had run the check lifted the paper with the result and held it in front of me with a grin. The man *was* the absconder from prison and he had a completely different name. I couldn't believe it and turned to face the man, seeking an explanation for his misrepresentation. The second the result came back, his demeanour completely changed and he turned into an arrogant, self-assured product of the prison system. He smirked at me and drawled, "Well, it was worth a shot, wasn't it, love?" I stood dumbfounded for a while as I thought of how I had so nearly been duped into releasing him because he was so convincing and how he had snapped from one personality to another, as if someone had just clicked their fingers. It turned out that the man he was impersonating was his twin brother, also involved in crime and somehow the descriptive details had been mixed up. I again resolved always to act on my gut instinct and never to leave loose ends.

My new Brighton team got on well together and we had a good mixture of experienced and new officers. We tried to have a team breakfast once a week for team bonding, attending a local café. On most occasions this was cut short due to emergency calls but occasionally we managed to finish. Unfortunately, one day a civilian took exception to the fact that we were taking a "team break". He burst in through the café door ranting and raving about abuse of power and that he paid our wages. We listened to him not really knowing how to respond until the most senior officer there, who had had his back to the man, turned around slowly and said calmly with a touch of annoyance, "Do you mind, I'm eating my breakfast!" as we all tried unsuccessfully to smother our giggles. This was the final straw for the man who stormed to the police station to make a complaint. Later our sergeant, who had received the man at the police station, asked us if in future we could seek out a less visible place to eat.

Having to eat on duty often caused these types of problems as people didn't always appreciate that we needed to eat as well. Due to the nature of our work we usually had to buy takeaways; there wasn't time to do any cooking or to prepare anything because of the crazy shifts we were working. Technically we had a forty-five minute food break but it was generally understood that this could be interrupted, postponed or cancelled for any type of emergency, and in Brighton there were many.

# CHAPTER THIRTEEN

# Fear of the Unknown

Unfortunately, after just a few months at Brighton, our new team was reduced in size from around sixteen officers to a mere eight due to transfers and other issues. Our team also suffered from a disproportionately high number of internal investigations, with officers at various points being removed from duty temporarily or required to resign or who were dismissed in the more serious cases. However, contrary to popular belief, I saw no evidence of widespread corruption or dishonesty throughout my service in the police. It was the individual officers who let us down and no one condoned them when they did. The vast majority of officers were diligently trying to do a difficult job, sometimes with few resources and a lack of support.

There are many incidents that stand out in my mind, as I remained at Brighton Central for over a year and it was always very busy. The hardest thing to deal with as a police officer is definitely the natural human fear of the unknown. I hated entering buildings or searching areas especially at night if I didn't know what I was likely to find. I became very jumpy and irrationally afraid of this type of thing which was obviously a big part of my job. Maybe I had watched one too many horror movies or my imagination was too active. It was definitely a problem.

One evening we received a call from a man stating that his next door neighbour was in his own back-garden scrabbling around and digging up the dirt with his bare hands. This was obviously odd behaviour and he wanted us to check it out. We arrived at the property to find the front door locked and nobody answering. I looked in through the front lounge window which was partially open and could see strange writing all over the walls inside the house. The place had been trashed, with clothes and rubbish everywhere. The back kitchen door was also open, with large piles of stuff stacked in the doorway in a chaotic fashion. I was immediately afraid of what we might find as clearly the man was suffering from some kind of mental health problem and I thought that he may have harmed himself or another person.

My colleague told me that as the smaller (and least senior) of the two of us, I would have to climb in through the lounge window and then let her in through the front door. I resisted at first, but I knew that she was right so eventually I plucked up the courage and climbed in with my heart beating rapidly. I was terrified that the man would suddenly appear and rush at me with some type of weapon as I couldn't see around the corner into the corridor leading to the front door. If he appeared now, I would be alone with a crazy man in a strange house, with what looked like satanic writing all over the walls. I rushed to the door breathing a sigh of relief as my colleague joined me; she was not very sympathetic and found my panic amusing.

We went outside to the garden but there was no one there. There were half buried dishes and other kitchen items in the garden. Then I saw the garden shed. Again I felt fear welling up inside me as I knew we would have to search it and I half expected to find the man dead inside. I held my breath as we opened the door, but the shed was empty so I exhaled rapidly. The two of us went back inside the house and walked upstairs where we found a ladder leading to a loft hatch. I knew I had to check inside the hatch but would rather have done anything else at that moment. As I climbed the ladder, I knew that my head would be exposed to whoever was up there or that I might see something horrible when I looked around. My colleague had to practically force me up the ladder as I was shaking like a leaf and felt ill. The suspense was too much for my nervous system. I climbed a few rungs on the ladder until my head was just below the opening then quickly looked up and around and ducked my head down again, all within half a second.

Gratefully, I came back down the ladder but my colleague said, "Natalie, when the sergeant asks you later if you are sure the house is empty, what are you going to say?" I just couldn't do it again, so my colleague took pity on me and checked instead. We then returned to the police station. When my sergeant heard what had happened he laughed but then said that I looked very pale and asked if I was okay. I said that I felt ill and that the incident had just been too strange for me as I dreaded what I might have found around every corner.

Despite my intense emotions, it was obviously necessary for us to continue attempting to locate the man. We were given an address of a friend of his and went to check if he was there. I was dreading locating the man because of the things I had seen at his house. I imagined he would be a raving lunatic who might try to attack us with a knife or other weapon as we struggled to wrestle him into our police vehicle bound for the nearest hospital. In trepidation I knocked on the door of the friend's house and waited anxiously until a man answered the door. The man who answered looked relatively normal with no trace of the psychotic wildness that I had built up in my mind. I assumed he was the friend until he confirmed that he was in fact our "missing" man.

Then followed a rather strange conversation as we discussed the events that had occurred at his own address only hours earlier where, amongst other things, he had been frantically digging up earth with his bare hands in order to bury his kitchenware and writing insane messages on his interior walls. He explained that he had had some kind of emotional and mental relapse due to complications with his medication and a relationship breakdown, but that he felt a lot better now that he was with his friend and away from the original environment. Meeting the man and seeing that he was now of sound mind diminished the fear I had felt before. However, on initially attending the friend's address, I had definitely not envisaged calmly meeting the man, chatting with him in the hallway for a brief period and then driving away to resume our duties. My sometimes irrational fear of the unknown was my biggest hurdle throughout my career.

The more sobering side of policing a place like Brighton is that we never really knew when we would be in danger, it being impossible to prepare for every eventuality. Once, a colleague and I somehow found ourselves trapped in a room with a guy who had pulled a knife halfway through our conversation and was now threatening to harm himself. He was a very big man and had mental health problems so there was no guarantee that he wouldn't turn on us. We had carelessly allowed him to get between us and the door, and now we were trapped. In the end we managed to talk him into handing over the knife, which was a great relief as it had been a really dangerous situation.

By far the worst incident involving one of our own officers was when two of our team attended a routine incident. They had been there a while when we heard a female colleague scream into the radio, followed quickly by the frightened shout, "Man with a knife," before there was a deathly silence. Then everything went crazy as we tried to establish a location to help our colleagues. Fortunately, our supervisors took control of the situation. A man had attacked the two officers with a knife and escaped from the building. One of the officers had a very slight nick to his head but the scary part was that the knife had left an indentation on his glasses where the offender had tried to slash his eye. His glasses protected him from worse damage.

This shook all of us up including the Chief Constable of the day, who mistakenly printed an article in the local police magazine saying how humbled he had been when he met the officers involved. This infuriated our sergeant as the Chief hadn't actually met the officers at all. Obviously he was pre-empting the meeting, thinking he would get there in time for the publication, but failed to do so. It was amusing watching our sergeant weighing up the pros and cons of sending an email to the Chief about how he felt about this publication. In the end he composed the email, waited for a few seconds and then verbally said goodbye to his career as he pressed "send".

# CHAPTER FOURTEEN

# The Lighter Side

Having a job like this and dealing with tragedy and violence day after day was obviously tough emotionally. It was imperative that we kept our sense of humour and learnt to laugh about both our mistakes and about incidents we dealt with. One of the most common mistakes officers made was to leave their email account open at their desk terminal when they left for a while, either because they had been forced to dash out to an incident mid-sentence or due to negligence. This was before the time when tampering with someone's email account became a disciplinary matter, so it was routine to send emails from an unsuspecting person's account to their sergeant telling them that they loved them or asking for promotion, or to more senior officers asking daft questions about divisional policy.

However, one of my colleagues took the joke too far one day when he sent a "lonely hearts" type email from my account to the entire force of over five thousand people. Apparently I was a "fun loving single looking for companionship and requesting immediate responses". I received around thirty replies and was pretty embarrassed about the whole thing, but could see the funny side. Unfortunately for the prankster, our supervision didn't, and made an exception in this case by treating the matter as disciplinary!

One of the most humorous incidents that I recall occurred when I was alone on routine patrol and was approached by a member of the public. I waited for the usual request for directions, or a complaint about a petty neighbourhood dispute, or harassment via social media or text message, but to my surprise the person said, "I think there's a dead body over there!"

This is a probationary officer's worst nightmare as at this stage in our training we just about had enough confidence to issue traffic tickets and public order warnings, but being the first officer at the scene of a potential murder in an area open to the public was far beyond my comfort zone! With trepidation, I walked across to where the person had pointed and, sure enough, I could see a male body lying with his head at the foot of a flight of stairs leading down into a basement. The body was covered in leaves and other rubbish and looked as if it had been there for some time. I couldn't see how a person lying at such an angle could possibly be alive, especially as the man's skin looked discoloured and grey. I couldn't reach him without disturbing the evidence of what I now believed to be a serious crime scene, as it would involve going through the basement gate and potentially dislodging the body.

Many people had gathered as we were still near the main high street and they waited with bated breath to see what I would do. I turned away from the body, my heart pounding and used my radio to call for an ambulance, supervision, and CID to come to the incident. At least I knew this part of the procedure, and with all these other people in attendance I wouldn't have to make any difficult decisions. This was all being organised when I heard a noise, like a muffled cough from behind me. I turned around to see that the "dead" body had risen from his temporary, and no doubt extremely uncomfortable, grave and was now standing looking totally bemused by all of the people staring at him. I was speechless at first but when I had recovered myself I said the only thing that came to me: "What are you doing?" "Sleeping," came the obvious reply, and, "What are *you* doing?" I didn't try to explain myself as I hastily cancelled all the extra resources I had requested and slipped away into the safety of the crowd.

I hoped rather than believed this would be the last of this incident but of course my sergeant and other colleagues wouldn't let this rest. For weeks after this I was asked on the radio whether I needed CID and an ambulance to join me at every incident I attended. My sergeant also frequently asked me if I needed him to come with me when attending routine shoplifting matters, and colleagues attending incidents where people had died called me to ask if I could assist them in checking the vital signs! It was a tough lesson to learn and I was amazed how quickly I had forgotten everything I had been taught in training at the first sign of a serious incident. My mind just went blank and common sense flew out of the window.

Occasionally I met someone in the course of my duties who made me laugh to the extent that I was unable to complete the task I was trying to accomplish. Usually this would be other colleagues, so it didn't matter so much, but once in a while it was a criminal who was probably trying to distract me from arresting him or her. I stopped a cyclist in a back alley in the centre of Brighton and was trying to establish his name. I didn't really think he would be known to the police for anything but he had cycled somewhere he wasn't meant to so I used the opportunity to check his details. He began spelling his name very slowly and deliberately and I repeated it back to him but as I spelt it back I realised he was spelling "Osama Bin Laden." He did this with a completely dead pan expression and no trace of humour, but for some reason it just struck me as very funny.

I looked at this seriously misguided person in front of me who had just given his name as (at the time) one of the world's most wanted and feared terrorists and said to him seriously, "Your name is Osama Bin Laden?" However, as I said it, my voice cracked and I couldn't contain the laughter as the situation was so ridiculous. This guy was acting as if he thought I would accept the name and let him go! He started laughing as well but every time I tried to get his name he said it again and I ended up in hysterics, which he also thought was funny. Unfortunately, my loss of control led to the guy disregarding my instruction to wait, and cycling off up the road. I was forced to call for back up as I wouldn't be able to catch him on foot. He was stopped just up the road by other officers who, not finding him so amusing, ascertained his correct details and found that there was an outstanding warrant for his arrest!

Another time I was present when a colleague was arresting a drunk person in the street. There were quite a few officers there dealing with him and we had attracted a bit of attention from the public. Another drunk man happened to walk past and made a comment in a rather posh accent about the situation even though it was nothing to do with him. He was warned about his language and in response said "What are you arresting him for? You [insert two four letter words]!" At this point, my colleague quite rightly grabbed him and said, "Right, you're coming in as well," and put him in the back of the van with the original man.

All the way to the custody centre, we could hear the two of them in the back of the van. The first man was drunkenly mumbling and the second man, who later turned out to be a barrister, was responding, "Don't talk to me, you're a drunk." There was a commotion as we arrived at the cell block as the barrister made his presence known loudly, partly because the other officers weren't used to hearing such a posh accent from a prisoner. We were all highly entertained as he was being booked in by the custody sergeant when he asked for the sergeant's last name. Then he asked him to spell it aloud. When the sergeant did this, the barrister asked him whether he might be a descendant in the line of Queen Anne before announcing that the sergeant was doing an excellent job and he was going to write to the Chief Constable about him. When the procedure was finished, he announced loudly, "Right then, carry on!" before waving his hand in the air as if he were royalty and stumbling away to the cell block as we all fell about laughing.

# CHAPTER FIFTEEN

# Weekends in West Street

One of the aspects of working in Brighton Central that I thought I would really hate, based on my previous experience in Public Order Training, was policing the city centre high street at the weekends in the evening. Public order really wasn't my thing; I was more the investigative type. My only experience of public order at this point was when I had been on standby to assist specially trained public order officers in a riot situation after a post football match drinking session got out of hand in Brighton centre. Apparently the two sets of rival supporters had somehow ended up in the same pub, clearly a big and costly mistake. I witnessed serious violence with windows being smashed and chairs thrown at my colleagues. Police dogs were going crazy as they were set on people, and batons and shields had to be used as the officers were pummelled with missiles. It was a terrifying situation and I was glad I could legitimately stand at a distance; being part of the back-up or reserve unit, I was not allowed to get involved unless instructed to do so. Fortunately, no officers were seriously injured in the end but the incident put me off public order for life.

However, the weekends policing West Street with my regular team were somewhat different and I actually grew to enjoy and look forward to them. The camaraderie in our team was at its best at these times; when we had enough staff, it wasn't so dangerous and it could actually be quite fun. Within our team, I didn't really have to do much in terms of physical restraint as this wasn't really my forte. One of my colleagues demonstrated this in the office by managing to handcuff me to a chair with my own handcuffs that he had taken from my kit belt before I knew what was happening. He made the point that I wouldn't fare very well if a criminal tried this and I pointed out that I shouldn't have to be on alert for criminals whilst in the police station! I was willing to use force when necessary but as the guys I worked with were more than happy to take on this role, most of the time I took a back seat. I even recall in the city centre one guy punching another whilst they were standing right next to me, and before I could react, some male officers were on top of the offender on the ground.

The downside of weekend policing was that it was totally pointless even attempting to buy hot food in our forty-five minute refreshment break as we always ended up abandoning it to attend an emergency. Nearly every weekend as we were preparing to leave at midnight from our late shifts, the radio call went out, "No officers to stand down without permission from..." A collective groan went up as this meant that we had to do compulsory overtime, usually until 3am. Several times this occurred, not because of the usual public order type incidents, but because a group of young children from a specific family had gone missing from the outskirts of Brighton and it was necessary for us to locate them. They always chose the busiest times to do this (the weekend) and after a few incidents we knew where to look: the hotels in the city centre. Unbelievably, these three children who were aged between six and twelve, dressed in their nightwear, with the youngest carrying a teddy bear, managed several times to get from outer Brighton to the centre and into the lobby of a hotel without raising an alarm. You can probably imagine the panic in the ranks of the senior officers when we first received a call of this nature.

The Brighton cell block was often full of prisoners, especially at weekends, and on one night the nearest alternative cell block space, being reserved for serious crime only, was at Hastings (one and a half hours away)! But I was young and had few responsibilities outside of work and mostly liked the opportunity to earn the extra money. One guy I knew worked double shifts for many months and completely cleared the mortgage on his house!

A few times things did get out of control as five to ten police officers attempted to keep the peace with thousands of drunk people milling around. The most annoying of these were the student lawyers and people who thought they knew the law as they drunkenly tried to tell us how to do our jobs. On the rare occasion we felt the need to respond with, "If you are a law student, you will know why I'm not going to do what you are telling me to do." Oh, and the people who shouted, "I pay your wages, so arrest him," in our faces; that was annoying, too.

One night a van of us arrived in West Street responding to a reported fight, only to find five separate groups of two or three people lying on the ground. On moving closer to one such group, I saw that one man was lying underneath another man, both on their backs, and the man underneath had the head of the man lying on top of him in a vice-like lock. The man on top was struggling to breathe so I shouted at the man underneath to release the headlock before he choked to death. Unbelievably, at this point the guy doing the choking shoved a door staff ID at me. He was a security officer at one of the clubs! As it turned out, all of the groups were in the same situation so we ended up arresting all of the door staff on suspicion of attempting to cause grievous bodily harm, as they couldn't provide a reasonable explanation for their behaviour. Later they were all sacked. We dealt with a number of incidents like this where door staff were heavy handed but it was important for us to remember the circumstances they were in and to support them where possible.

On another occasion, a senior colleague lost his temper with a group of people involved in some type of public order incident. He threatened to spray the crowd with Captor if they didn't disperse peacefully. Captor is basically pepper spray. All officers carried it and were trained to spray it into the face of a non-compliant person. It causes extreme pain, with the person's eyes closing and their face screwing up, giving the officer enough time to force compliance, usually through handcuffing or another approved technique. Some officers were a bit "Captor happy", using it more regularly than others, but in general it was used appropriately. I only used mine once during my entire police service, preferring to try to talk people down rather than wind them up for a fight.

This officer, however, had a reputation for using his Captor spray a lot, so much so that in the station he had been given a fire extinguisher with his name and "Captor spray" written on it as a joke by the rest of the guys in our team. The officer also had a reputation for not always doing as he was told. I remember once standing in my inspector's office and saw him do a double-take as he looked at the CCTV feed which was showing an area of the town. He then exploded with annoyance as he identified the officer on camera and said that he had just told him not to go out on patrol wearing a certain item of non-police issue uniform, yet here he was as clear as day, less than thirty minutes after the instruction, wearing it proudly as if the conversation hadn't even taken place!

I was standing next to this officer in the high street as he made a threat to use his Captor spray and then carried it out when two guys stepped towards him. He sprayed a whole crowd of people with the stuff. Afterwards, some of the targets, led by their friends as they couldn't see properly, wandered off up the street with tears pouring down their faces. But the officer didn't stop there. He shouted at the crowd asking if anyone else "wanted some", and when one guy moved, he reached for the spray again. I realised I should do something about this as I could see that it was getting out of hand and that we weren't achieving anything. So I nervously (as this was a more senior officer) put my hand on his arm and suggested that maybe we should try to arrest the original offender rather than emptying the rest of his Captor spray into the crowd. I think this snapped him back to reality as to my relief he forgot about the provocation of the now very angry group and stepped in to arrest the original offender.

Afterwards, I didn't really know what to do about what had happened, as Captor shouldn't be sprayed into a group of people; it is meant for dealing with individuals with due consideration being given to the aftercare. Most of the crowd that had been sprayed had wandered off with no aftercare whatsoever! Fortunately, incidents like this were rare and most officers used their Captor sparingly.

The most disgusting incident I witnessed was as we were driving a patrol car in West Street and I saw out of the car window a man leaning up against the wall and committing a sex act on himself in broad daylight in the high street with many people milling around. Fortunately, I was with a male colleague and as I reacted to what I had just seen, he also saw what was going on and we both got out of the car to deal with the man. My colleague took the lead and said to him, "Put it away, mate, there's people here!" which I thought summed up the situation well. He was later charged with the common law offence of "Outraging Pubic Decency", which he definitely had!

The craziest idea from a senior member of staff, whilst I was working at Brighton, was to make a pledge to the public that there would be an officer stationed twenty-four hours a day at the clock tower in Brighton centre. The officer would change every hour. Why is this crazy? Because it created total havoc on the ground, especially when trying to change over. Brighton is a place that is always busy and there are barely enough officers to cover all of the incidents being reported. Sometimes I arrived for work on a Friday or Saturday night to find there were ten emergencies that hadn't been resourced (no one had been sent to them). These were not general queries, but incidents of stabbing, domestic assaults and other violent crime. You get the point, Brighton is busy.

Removing one officer from a team which sometimes only had five to begin with really wasn't helpful. Although the sergeant diligently handed out the clock tower duties at the beginning of each shift, this was normally scrapped after the first hour of mayhem because someone wasn't where they were meant to be, either due to an incident they were involved in or by design as they hated the duty. Either way officers ended up doing the proposed one hour clock tower duty for anything up to six hours on some nights.

Having a clock tower officer helped to create crime, when the officer standing guard was assaulted or provoked by a homeless person wanting a bed for the night. The officer being present also assisted in the reporting of incidents that otherwise wouldn't have come to police attention, because they were at the centre of things and inevitably witnessed them! Being an upright citizen you may think this is a good thing, but on a Friday night low level crime is the least of the police priorities and it would be much better if these things were left to work themselves out on their own. Then there was the graveyard shift between 4am and 7am where there wasn't a single soul around and the officer had to stand there come rain or shine or in freezing temperatures wishing they could watch paint dry instead as that would have been more interesting. Needless to say the idea was scrapped in the end.

The most blatant criminal activity I recall was a burglary and criminal damage at 6am, all captured on CCTV. It occurred at the bottom of West Street next to the beach area. We were completing paperwork back at the police station after a busy night and preparing for handover at 7am, not really expecting any additional incidents. On being alerted by a CCTV operator to a crime in progress, we took a quick look at the CCTV in the office before attendance. Unbelievably, two men were, in broad daylight and making no attempt to hide what they were doing, smashing all of the club windows and removing black bin liners full of bottles of alcohol from the interior. They must have realised they would be caught or were too drunk to care. Both men were still at the scene when we arrived. We arrested them, but one of the men, who was 6'8", somehow managed to get his handcuffs from behind him to the front without me noticing, whilst in the police car, which was only one of many strange things about this guy. He had only appeared in Brighton a week before and I had seen him nearly every day, usually in strange circumstances. After this incident he mysteriously disappeared from the area.

Being a young female officer in uniform and working in a place like Brighton brought me an undue amount of male attention. I didn't mind the odd bit of flirting and the odd comment as long as it was not crude, but there was one guy who went a bit too far one evening. After obtaining my first name from a willing colleague, he began following me around in the high street begging me to arrest him. He even got down on his knees holding his hands out for handcuffs. However, as I tried to walk away from this guy, he wasn't having any of it. He managed to get inside a moving van with its side door open and then instructed the driver to drive slowly down the high street next to me as I walked, whilst he proclaimed his undying love for me to all at the top of his voice. I was so embarrassed, but my colleagues thought it was hilarious and encouraged him to continue. He eventually gave up when I made it really clear I wasn't interested and stopped being nice to him.

I generally avoided the people who deliberately tried to get themselves arrested. We had a few homeless people who threatened to commit a minor crime in order to get a bed for the night; we didn't want to encourage this so we tended just to walk away from them as quickly as possible, or run if necessary. The persistent ones found themselves temporarily placed into the back of the nearest police van and driven some distance away before being removed and told to walk the long journey back to wherever it was they had started. This practice was, probably quite rightly, stopped in the end as those who had taken part over the years reached higher ranks and were concerned about the prospect of being sued if some harm were to come to the individual due to the involuntary transfer.

# CHAPTER SIXTEEN

# When Everything Falls Apart

I enjoyed my job and made the most of the limited time off. But socially I was off the rails drinking, smoking and gambling whenever I got the opportunity. I thought about my former Christian beliefs at times and couldn't shake them off completely but surrounded myself with distractions.

In August 2002 everything fell apart when our family suffered its greatest and most difficult loss: my younger brother James was killed in a car accident near to the family home at the age of just eighteen. Within a week of the funeral, my relationship with my boyfriend broke down largely due to the intense pressure of the trauma of it all. Those were dark days as after just a week of compassionate leave, I returned to work on the understanding that I could take more time off later at short notice, if required. I went through the motions at work as I felt the physical pain of the double loss for months. I was grateful to the few people who tried to support me at this time. I especially remember one of my work colleagues taking me out for a coffee and relating a far worse tragedy that had occurred in her life when she had been a lot younger.

Over time things did get easier and I threw myself back into my work. I advised my supervisors that I didn't want to attend the scene of any serious car accidents for the foreseeable future and they said they would do their best but if I was the only officer available, I would have to go. I knew my colleagues would rally round and stop this from happening as other officers had things they avoided or struggled to deal with and we all helped out. I hadn't realised it but I wasn't ready to be back at work, due to my brother's death. I was in the office one evening a few months after the accident when a call came in from a man stating that he had been having a party in his fourth floor flat and that someone had fallen out of the window to the ground below. He said that all he could see on the ground was a kettle the man had been holding when he fell. I volunteered to attend this incident with my colleague, not really thinking too much about it but knowing it wouldn't be pleasant. My sergeant asked me if I was sure I would be okay and I responded that I wanted to get it over with. In the car on the way there I mentally prepared myself for dealing with a dead body and with distraught friends.

We arrived at the scene and were confronted by a man obviously distressed who stated he had made the call. He told us that there were twenty people still dancing upstairs. We said we would look for the man who had fallen first. We started to check the ground and I saw the kettle. I began to feel uncomfortable as we continued checking what was a very small area with no trace of the body. My fear of the unknown reared its ugly head again as we decided to go with the man up to his flat to speak to the other people and get more information. The man continued talking to us as we walked, clearly distressed but appearing lucid and rational. I began shaking as we walked up the stairs as something wasn't quite right; I had been preparing myself to deal with a body and then it wasn't there. The whole thing was very strange and my brain couldn't deal with the change of circumstances.

My colleague entered the flat first to find it empty; there were no people dancing. She began searching the room as the man commented that it was strange as there had been people there just a minute ago. As my colleague opened a floor to ceiling door, a huge object fell out and I screamed. It was a big roll of carpet but I had thought it was a dead body. I began to cry as I backed out of the flat and began walking back down the stairs. I found it difficult to walk as I continued to navigate the stairs.

Then I saw that many more officers including an inspector had arrived and were waiting for us to come out. This is normal for this type of incident and I knew the inspector. She was very kind as she had been on duty when my brother had died and she knew that this was part of the reason for my reaction. She ushered me to a car away from prying eyes as I explained through tears that I just hadn't been prepared for this strange type of incident. She arranged for another officer to take me home and I asked for an update with the outcome of the incident. Later an officer phoned to tell me that the man had been arrested and taken to the station for his own safety under the Mental Health Act.

Shortly after this I attended an accidental death of a forty-year-old man. His parents were there when we arrived and were obviously upset. This didn't impact me too badly at first as I went through the various procedures. When I was alone with the mother, I offered her my own experience of losing my brother and how it had impacted our family. She was grateful for the humanity that I showed, asking me how my own mother had dealt with the loss. This was a judgement call as it could be seen as highly inappropriate to bring my own trauma into this situation but I felt it might be helpful to the lady. After this, the father managed to reach a relative he had been trying to get hold of and began weeping into the phone as he told the story. I couldn't cope with this and had to leave the room as my own tears came. I couldn't go back into that house afterwards and had to leave my colleague to deal with the family.

During the period that I was still struggling with grief, a new officer joined our team. We became good friends as I could see that he was looking out for me within the team and helping me at work where he could. Due to recent events I was struggling to get through every day at work and had become de-motivated and lacked the work ethic I had had before. This new officer was immediately popular in the team as he had some experience with a previous police force, which appealed to the more experienced officers who were fed up with working with many probationary officers and having to teach us everything.

However, over time I became a bit uncomfortable around this guy due to a few things that he had said and done and the inexplicable feeling that things were not quite as they seemed. I moved departments during this period and was no longer working directly with him, which helped put some distance to our friendship. I didn't think much more about the situation until I was visited one day in my new department by my previous supervisor. He told me that my former friend had just resigned! He asked me how close we had been as he knew that we had been friends. I explained that more recently I had been trying to keep away from him as he made me uneasy but that I didn't really know my reason for feeling like this. The sergeant then dropped a bombshell. He told me that everything this guy had said about his life and prior work experience had been a lie. He had basically made up his entire life and one of the lies he had told outside of work had caught up with him at work resulting in his downfall.

I was caught totally off guard by this revelation as although I had felt that something wasn't quite right, I would never have guessed the extent of the deception. I trusted this guy and had confided in him a lot in recent months. I felt really strange as I thought back over conversations we had had. I recalled one that I had initiated about honesty and how important it was to me in my friendships, thinking of course that everyone wanted honest friendships. The guy reacted as if I had punched him in the face and after recovering himself he said by way of explanation simply that my comments had "knocked him for six". I should have realised then that something was amiss!

When I look back now I see the hand of God in this whole situation moving me away from this guy pretending to be my friend who wasn't who he seemed to be at a point when I was especially vulnerable due to losing two important people in my life at the same time. Even though I had turned my back on God and wasn't interested in Him, He was still protecting me.

# CHAPTER SEVENTEEN

# A Step Closer

In the back of my mind throughout my first two years was my long-term ambition to become a detective working with the Criminal Investigation Department (CID). My transfer to Brighton made this more of a possibility as they were very short of qualified detectives. I was advised that I could apply for the Trainee Detective Constable (TDC) procedure as soon as I had finished my two year probationary period as a uniformed officer.

I mentioned in the previous chapter that I moved to another department; I actually moved into the CID department as a uniformed attachment pending my application for the TDC procedure. One of the first things I noticed was that there was a wall in the CID office with various pieces of paper on it. These were copies of witness statements and reports written by uniformed officers that had amused the detectives. My favourite examples were, "We didn't arrest them because they were in their pyjamas and ready for bed," and, "I turned to my colleague and said to him in code that the male should be arrested." I knew I was going to like working with CID.

I spent a lot of my time on attachment to CID working on one case which turned into one of the biggest disappointments of my career. It was a case of multiple thefts at a local gym. The offender broke into lockers, stealing credit cards and cash, and then used the cards to purchase expensive items. The gym had a swipe card system allowing entry so I knew he or she had to be a member. I set about examining the dates and times of the swipes to establish the most likely suspect and also obtained lists of the transactions on the credit cards. I used the lists to identify specific stores where the offender had used the cards and then tried to identify him on CCTV in the stores. Eventually, I managed to obtain a photo from the CCTV of a person using one of the cards at the till. I took it to the gym and asked staff if they knew who it was. They were gob-smacked as this was a regular attendee who was also friendly with the staff.

We arrested the man and conducted a lengthy search at his house. Nearly all of the items there matched items purchased on the stolen credit cards with a few having almost unique batch numbers matching the numbers on the credit card receipts. This guy had filled his house with these expensive items of clothing, electronics and other things. He didn't say anything in the police interview and I was forced to place him on bail. He had no prior record with the police, which surprised me; in fact he didn't seem to behave like a typical criminal at all. I could see how he had befriended the people at the gym as he was very plausible. If it weren't for the overwhelming evidence against him, I would have believed that I had made a mistake, but at his house I also found an expired membership card for another gym and decided to pay them a visit. They advised me that they had previously cancelled his membership as they suspected him of thieving, which confirmed my suspicions.

Eventually this guy was charged with most of the thefts based on the CCTV footage and the circumstantial evidence connecting him to the other thefts due to the property found at his house. As the file was being prepared for court, I received an urgent message. The CCTV tape and main evidence from the case file, which all had been in one bundle, were missing and the prosecutor planned to drop the case if it couldn't be found. We searched everywhere for that evidence to no avail so the case was dropped and the suspect was advised no further action would be taken against him. We still had a room full of the property that I believed he had stolen using the cards and this all had to be returned to him as we couldn't prove it wasn't his. He later made a complaint that his property had been damaged during storage and, to add insult to injury, I believe he was given a financial compensation settlement.

After all of this, a few months later, the missing CCTV tape and paperwork were left on my desk one day by an unknown person with just a handwritten note that they had found it somewhere. I knew that I couldn't do anything about it now as it was too late. I had spent months working on this case alone and I was devastated by the outcome and the possibility that someone in the police station may have been working against me. My seniors were none too impressed and took this failure as evidence that I wasn't quite up to the task which also annoyed me as I was convinced the case had been deliberately sabotaged. I had to put this case behind me and move on.

During my attachment I was given the task of sorting through reports of crime that were being held by uniformed officers and establishing how they could be progressed more efficiently. Being highly organised and enjoying extra responsibility, I really enjoyed this role. I also liked the opportunity to shock the detective inspector (DI) every so often by knocking on his door and advising him that I had found another "CID" job that had been languishing in the tray of a uniformed officer for far too long. As CID only investigated crimes of a serious nature, the policy was that the initial investigation by the uniformed officers would be completed within twenty-four hours and the report would then be passed straight to CID for secondary investigation. However, things do not always go to plan, as was obviously the case when I found a report of a robbery that had occurred at least one month previous, during which two victims were attacked with a variety of different weapons and later one had suffered a collapsed lung. The DI's face was a picture as he immediately grabbed the report from me and started arranging resources to deal with the matter.

# CHAPTER EIGHTEEN

# A Childhood Dream Fulfilled

I passed the CID exam in November 2003 and became an official plain clothed detective. I was assigned to one of the CID teams and, due to the lack of staff, was immediately bombarded with case files, including a child abduction and rape investigation, that I had no idea how to progress. It took me a while to find my feet and I struggled a lot with the workload and expectations. I was still just twenty-two and mostly working with older officers.

The cases I worked on always seemed to go wrong at court, including one that caught the attention of the media as it involved the Brighton Gay Pride event. A staff member was accused of embezzling funds over a long period of time but claimed it was to make up for a lack of proper pay. The court accepted his explanation and he was found not guilty. In another of my cases, a verbal confrontation between strangers resulted in a man being stabbed, but the suspect claimed self-defence. He was found guilty of a lesser crime than the original charge and received a suspended prison sentence due to his personal circumstances.

Honestly, neither of these cases affected me in a negative way as I knew from the outset they could go either way and although as police officers we are to be impartial when gathering evidence, we still have feelings and convictions about the right outcome. In both cases I was concerned that the suspects might be convicted unfairly so in the circumstances the outcomes seemed fair.

I worked on another case, however, that did affect me and caused a great deal of frustration. I was investigating a series of robberies at betting shops in the area, including one where a member of staff had resisted and been stabbed. The witnesses in a few of the robberies stated that there was something distinctive about the offender's face. I was able to link the current series of thefts to unsolved robberies dating back over previous years due to the description of the suspect and the *modus operandi*, or method of operation, used.

I received a handwritten letter identifying the offender using only his street name, but the information came from the criminal underworld and couldn't therefore be used in an official capacity, although it did assist me with my investigation. On police databases, there was a mass of intelligence relating to serious criminal activity under the street name I had been given, and I wondered who I was dealing with. The intelligence officers at Brighton were also keen to identify the person but we only had a street name loosely connected to a list of unsolved crimes and no clue as to the true identity of the person.

Eventually a name was suggested by another police force based on the distinctive facial feature of the suspect. This man had previous convictions for robbery and was already wanted for a robbery at a building society in Hove dating back two years. This robbery had also been part of a series. The man had been in a group of youths who jumped over security screens and threatened violence in order to grab cash, leaving witnesses terrified. He had originally been arrested when his DNA was found on an item of clothing left at the scene. He was subsequently charged to appear at court for trial but was bailed and then failed to appear at court. He had been wanted by the police for over two years.

Due to the distinctive facial features of the man and the fact he had been wearing a face mask during the robberies, it would not be possible to place him on an identification procedure with the witnesses from the robberies because it wasn't possible to find other people who looked enough like him. I also explored the possibility of facial mapping, a new scientific technique comparing the structure of the face from CCTV images with the actual face of the suspect in custody. This was ruled out and I had to find another way to connect the man to his street name. I obtained a photo of the man and took it to someone who knew him only under his street name. The person confirmed that they knew the man in the photo and gave his street name. This confirmed that the two were one and the same. It was a massive breakthrough and solved the mystery of the elusive man but we still didn't know where he was or how to locate him. He was obviously good at hiding, having been missing for over two years whilst still involved in crime!

Searches were carried out at addresses connected to the man in an attempt to locate him. Finally, the persistence paid off when the suspect got fed up with the police hassling his friends and family. I arrived for work one day to be informed that the suspect had handed himself in at a police station in London on the original arrest warrant for the robbery from 2001. He had taken all of his belongings with him obviously believing he was going to prison. He was transported to Sussex where I interviewed him about the new series of robberies. He denied any involvement in any of the robberies and denied being connected to his street name although he admitted knowing the person who had identified him in the photo.

He appeared at court for a date to be set for his trial for the 2001 robbery and, unbelievably, the judge granted him bail again! I began to prepare for the trial but found that one of the key witnesses, a worker at the building society, had been so traumatised by the robbery that she was still suffering from post-traumatic stress disorder and had not only moved to a different job but also a different house in a different area. This really upset me and made me determined to make sure that justice was done if the woman agreed to testify, which she bravely did.

Meanwhile, the evidence in relation to the new series of robberies was being reviewed by the Crown Prosecution Service. If we charged the suspect, we would be relying on the testimony of a man from the criminal underworld who may have been involved in planning the attacks as he knew so much about them, and a young person who might be put at risk if they agreed to give evidence. We did everything we could to try to prove a link between the man and his street name, even attending a club event he was meant to be hosting. On arrival, there was a sign on the door stating the event had been postponed, no doubt because someone had tipped him off! In the end a decision was made not to prosecute the man as one witness lacked credibility and the other was too vulnerable. Now it was imperative that he be convicted on the original matter or he would walk out of court a free man.

The trial took place in 2004. The suspect was found guilty by the jury and later sentenced by the judge to four years' imprisonment. I was relieved that all of my hard work hadn't been for nothing and that this dangerous individual was finally behind bars. The action was also preventative as our string of betting shop robberies abruptly stopped.

# CHAPTER NINETEEN

# Significant Experiences

In my early days in CID I made a serious mistake, the consequences of which could have been severe. A colleague and I were dealing with a drunk person who was alleging that he had been raped. This person was known regularly to make this type of allegation but on the off-chance that he actually had been raped, we were duty bound to investigate fully every time. My colleague had gone elsewhere in the police station and I was sitting with the man writing down some basic details in the lobby area. My handbag, containing the car keys for our CID vehicle parked just outside, was on the chair between us. I turned around for just a few seconds to speak to a colleague but when I turned back to continue taking details from the man, he had vanished.

I didn't think much of this as it was the type of behaviour usually exhibited by him. I felt a bit irritated as I knew that now the allegation had been made, we, or someone from the next CID shift, would have to locate him in order to finalise the matter one way or another. My colleague returned and asked me where the man had gone. I told him what had happened as we headed out of the station intending to drive to another incident.

At the same moment, we both looked over towards our CID vehicle across the road and then my colleague made a loud exclamation as he had seen movement inside the vehicle. To my horror, I suddenly realised that the drunk man was inside our CID car in the driving seat with the keys in the ignition. I felt sick to my stomach as we frantically tried the doors only to find they were locked. We were then forced to rely on the goodwill of the drunk man to let us back into the vehicle and not to drive off up the road in our car. I knew my job would be on the line if we didn't succeed in persuading him, especially if he drove off and hurt himself or someone else. There was some negligence on my part as he had taken the keys from my bag. To my relief, my colleague remained calm and used his authoritative manner to persuade the man to let us into the vehicle. I was required to buy doughnuts for our team later (a punishment for stupid mistakes or lateness), but in the circumstances felt I had got off quite lightly considering the potential outcome.

One case that upset me and played on my mind afterwards was a serious assault that hadn't been reported at the time. We visited one of the victims after his mother contacted us to say that he had just been released from hospital having suffered a bleed on the brain due to an earlier head injury. After working on this case I understood why our CID supervisors were obsessive about making sure that any assaults with potential head injuries, even minor ones, were thoroughly investigated and why the victims were placed under a lot of pressure to go to hospital to be checked over. A lot of head injuries were presented as minor but internally it was a different story as injuries developed and progressed. It was not uncommon to arrive for a CID shift to discover that someone who had been the victim of a minor assault a week before had suddenly had an emergency admission to Hurstwood Park Neurological Unit and was now fighting for their life.

The reason this case upset me was because the male victim was young, maybe just seventeen. He and his two friends were at a local park when they were attacked by another group. All three were knocked unconscious with a range of weapons including a baseball bat and a metal bar. When they revived, the others had left the scene. Our victim went home to bed with only a dull headache but his mum found him the next day bleeding from his head and rushed him to hospital. His head injuries were serious and life changing and we could tell from speaking with him that he had suffered some type of brain injury. His mum told us how he had changed from a lively, fun loving boy to someone who was quiet, withdrawn, frequently moody and irritable, afraid to go out and suffering from depression.

I couldn't put out of my mind the lack of life I had seen in the eyes of this boy. I thought often about him and how meaningless the attack had been. I realised how fragile life was and how easy it was to sustain life changing injuries in a split second. Despite our best efforts, the attackers were never identified, which made it a lot worse in my view as no one had been brought to justice and there was no media interest in the story. It was as if nothing had happened in the eyes of the world, but one boy's life and the life of his family had been changed forever – and that should surely matter to someone?

After I had been in CID for a while there was a sudden mass exodus of officers to London due to the better pay and conditions being offered. I considered this myself several times but was worried about the long commute. We had to work a lot of overtime to cover the vacancies and many officers became de-motivated. Work life began to impinge on home life in an unacceptable way. I was at an all-night party on one of my days off; I had been drinking earlier in the night and had just gone to sleep at 5am when I received a call requesting I go into work. I protested, saying that I had been drinking and hadn't had any sleep. The response was, "I don't care; the boss wants everyone here as someone's been stabbed to pieces." Most officers switched their work phones off when they weren't on duty but I never quite managed to do this as it just felt wrong somehow.

This craziness continued for some time until I was suddenly informed that I was to be forcibly transferred to another department for three to six months to cover a vacancy. This was on a rotation so that every officer would take their turn, but I was the first as it would be "good experience for me as a trainee detective constable". My new department was Child Protection. I couldn't think of anything worse; I wasn't even sure whether or not I liked children, having had no real experience interacting with them, and felt I wasn't qualified to help people with children when I didn't have any of my own. People often commented that I looked too young to be a police officer and I was sure it would be even worse in this department.

## CHAPTER TWENTY

# Child Protection Team (CPT)

From the outset I was determined not to enjoy this role. I made it clear that as soon as I had done my time, which I saw almost as a prison sentence, I would be heading back to CID. However, having told my new boss how I felt, I agreed to his request to give things a chance and to work to the best of my ability. This was good advice and a good decision as CPT turned out to be my favourite department and in the end I stayed there for eighteen months by voluntary extension. I loved the less supervised working environment and the high workloads. I felt that I was really making a difference by helping children and families. I also enjoyed being the only on-duty CPT staff member during some weekends and making the decisions about any matters that arose.

During one of my first weekends the police received a call stating that there was a domestic dispute occurring at an address. I was monitoring the logs and recognised the address as one that belonged to a couple with a baby with whom CPT had had recent involvement. I checked their family file and found clear recent instructions, stating that if there was any further violence in the household, a court order would be obtained for the child to be removed. The woman had been informed that she needed to prove that she was trying to protect the child from any violence she received from the man by supporting any police investigations. The instruction to the police was that we should remove the baby from any violent situation using a police protection order.

Therefore, I established contact with the officers who had attended the address before and relayed the information. They said that the woman had been there alone with the baby and that the man had already left when they arrived. The woman had refused to provide a police statement and didn't want to report an assault although they had seen red marks on her neck. The officers left the premises.

I advised them that we needed to re-attend the address and speak to the woman again to make sure that she was safe, as the man was likely to return. On arrival, the woman came to the door carrying her baby; I spoke to her with the uniformed officers standing behind me. I explained that we needed to come inside the flat to check her welfare and that we would need to take the baby into police protection unless she was willing to accompany us to the police station to tell us what had happened and provide a witness statement. In reality we wouldn't want to get into a physical struggle in this situation so I needed the woman to hand the baby to us voluntarily or to come with us.

Without any warning she suddenly slammed the door on us and ran up the stairs inside the premises. The flat was on the second or third floor. I was extremely concerned for the welfare of the baby and the woman, especially as I had had them in my sights and had inadvertently let them go. I knew that whatever happened next was partly my responsibility, but I also knew that the woman was unlikely to harm her own baby.

After a few minutes delay we had the equipment needed to force an entry into the premises to ensure the welfare of both the woman and the baby. We ran up the stairs and into the flat, where the woman was standing alone looking disconcerted and uncomfortable, shifting from one foot to the other. I shouted at her to tell us where the baby was as I was afraid that she had done something really bad. The flat was small and as we raced around searching every nook and cranny for the baby my attention was suddenly drawn to the large open window leading out onto nearby rooftops. By this point I knew that the baby was not in the flat; my heart lurched as I briefly considered the possibility that the woman may have dropped her own baby out of the window rather than surrender it to the police. She was distressed but not enough to have killed her baby and she was shouting at me, "Where is the baby, where is the baby, can't you think about anything else?" Then we were informed by radio that a neighbour had seen a man jumping across rooftops and shimmying down a drainpipe with a bundle tucked down the front of his trousers.

Immediately the police helicopter was scrambled and every available officer deployed to the area to search for this man and the baby. I felt like I was watching a movie as events unfolded in front of me. I thought things couldn't get any worse as I finally managed to persuade the woman to give us a witness statement in relation to the original assault. I made it clear that there wasn't an alternative for her. Back at the police station I hid in my office in a daze as I contemplated the possible outcomes. I was very grateful when the highest ranking officer on the ground came to see me as I wanted to get any criticism over with. I started to apologise for my part in what had happened, but he immediately cut me off, stating that I had done the right thing in the circumstances and that the man's subsequent actions were in no way my fault. He pointed out that the reckless behaviour of the man was clear evidence that he was a danger to both the mother and the baby and that it was good that we had intervened when we had as he might have killed the woman otherwise. I still felt terrible but was glad that I wasn't going to be blamed for the sequence of events.

A few days later the man was detained in another part of the country for driving whilst disqualified with the baby in his car. He was later sentenced to three years in prison for recklessly endangering the life of a child and details of the story were all over the news. I still wasn't sure how my supervisors in CPT would react when they heard what had happened as they had not been on duty at the weekend. However, my boss called me into his office to thank me for the intervention, advising me that he was impressed that I had recognised the address at such an early stage and that I knew exactly what was required to be done. I was reassured and relieved to be backed up as officers making decisions in the heat of the moment were not always supported at a later stage. I wondered if the response would have been different if something had happened to the baby.

# CHAPTER TWENTY-ONE

# Hair Raising

One of the worst moments in my career occurred whilst I was working in CPT. To be honest, it was probably also one of the worst moments in the careers of many others working in or around my department on that day. Unfortunately, what happened was totally, utterly and completely my fault.

It started when I was asked to attend the Social Services office to interview a boy who had somehow ended up there. When I arrived, the boy gave a name that wasn't on our records and said that he was sixteen. The reason for police involvement was that he alleged that he had been kidnapped and detained for a few days by a group of men. I questioned him about the details of the "kidnapping" and almost immediately believed he was lying due to his mannerisms and the details that he was providing. His story about what had happened kept changing; he avoided eye contact with me and became belligerent as I talked to him. Then he stopped talking and refused to speak to me. I was getting irritated as I felt he was wasting police and Social Services' time.

However, I was not expecting him suddenly to get up and make a dash for the exit door of the building. This was where I made my big mistake as he had to run through several doors to get out and I really didn't do enough to stop him. This was partly because I believed him to be sixteen and therefore wasn't sure whether I had any power in law to detain him. A few social workers looked on helplessly as I followed him outside. By the time I got outside, he was disappearing around a corner and I knew I wouldn't catch him. I phoned my supervisor on the way back to the office to tell her what had happened. To my surprise, she was a bit annoyed with me and said that I shouldn't have allowed him to leave, but she also recognised there was nothing we could do about it now as he had already gone.

On arriving back at my desk at CPT, I quickly checked my emails and opened one that was marked as "urgent". I think the email had been sent to every officer in the country, which was unusual as a high clearance level was required to do this. As the email continued to open, I saw that the main content was a large colour picture of a male child. As I looked at the picture, I realised with horror that it was the boy who had just run away from me at the Social Services office. I felt the colour drain from my face as I continued reading that he was just twelve years old, had run away from a different part of the country and was considered to be at high risk of coming to harm. He had given me a false name which is why the "missing" marker hadn't flagged up when his name was checked.

Thinking this was definitely the end of a promising career, I did what I knew I had to do and informed my supervisor of the latest unfortunate development; I watched as the blood drained from her face as well. In fact this was to be a recurring theme as the information was passed further and further up the chain of command. After that everything went crazy as every available officer was deployed to search for the boy as senior officers tried in vain to explain to the other forces that he was still missing despite the fact that we had had him in our custody and he had somehow managed to escape. The kidnapping allegations didn't help matters as it was now a distinct possibility that I had enabled his "kidnappers" to re-capture him. The fact that the allegations were probably false was neither here nor there at this stage as everyone rushed around like a scene from Dad's Army, telling each other not to panic.

Several hours later at the point where anyone with even a small connection to the investigation was on the verge of suffering a permanent nervous breakdown, someone (who will be my best friend forever) found the boy and I was quickly driven to his location to verify his identity. He tried to run away again when he saw me as I was pretty upset with him, but this didn't matter as about ten officers surrounded him ensuring that this time he would be returned safely to his desperately worried family. I experienced a strange mixture of emotions for a child I barely knew as I wanted to hug him tightly and never let him go, but also to tell him off for lying and running away, leading us all on a not-so-merry dance, but also I felt the tears of relief welling up as I had been carrying the burden of the whole fiasco and the potential consequences for some five or six hours.

Afterwards, I think everyone involved knew that I had been punished enough by the thought of what would happen if we didn't locate the boy. Sometimes officers dropped the ball and, unfortunately, it tended to be the final outcome that determined the level of support they were given. I was just grateful that everyone dropped everything for the search and for the happy conclusion that was by no means guaranteed.

I mentioned in an earlier chapter that there had been a rush of officers transferring to the Metropolitan Police (MET) in London. After I had been working in CPT in Brighton for over a year, I decided to use my experience to apply for a role in CPT in London. Initial enquiries suggested my application would be looked on with favour as I had recently been trained in video interviewing both adults and children for sexual offences and had a variety of other sought-after skills. I had also just been confirmed in my rank of Detective Constable, having now completed my two year training period. I'm not totally sure of my underlying reasons for wanting to go but I was partly motivated by the wage increase and also the greater opportunities for specialisation within CPT in the MET. Although I had filled out my transfer request form which had been signed by my supervisors, I obviously wasn't totally convinced about the idea; when my detective inspector asked me to reconsider my transfer request on the basis that I was a valuable asset within the department at Brighton, I changed my mind virtually on the spot. Maybe I needed the affirmation but hadn't even realised it myself! I settled back down in CPT, quickly forgetting my former desire to transfer, which I'm now convinced would have been a complete disaster in any event.

After this, I dealt with a sensitive matter involving a young boy who was making an allegation that his teacher had physically assaulted him. The teacher had a good reputation at the school and had given an account to explain what had happened. I went to the family home with a social worker to talk to the boy. Bizarrely, one of the first things I noticed was that a fish tank in a prominent place in the house was completely covered in green algae and obviously hadn't been cleaned for a long time. I felt irrationally sorry for the fish swimming around inside the tank.

To begin with, the boy's mother was present as we spoke to him but she kept intervening in our dialogue and I could tell that we weren't going to get to the truth with her present, so we asked her to leave. She hovered nearby and was still listening to the discussion. When the boy started to admit that maybe things hadn't occurred as he had first remembered them, the mother exploded back into the conversation, fuming with anger, and said we were putting words in her son's mouth. I felt sorry for her in one respect because I knew that she believed that her son had been assaulted and that she was just trying to protect him, but we also had to think about the teacher's reputation. We tried to reason with her but she just got more and more angry. Throughout our discussion, I kept seeing the dirty fish tank out of the corner of my eye and although it had nothing to do with our visit, it really bothered me, so much so that as the woman finally ordered us to leave her house, I blurted out, "Oh, and you need to do something about that fish tank as well." The woman shouted, "What are you – the animal welfare department now, too?"

When I got back to the police station, my boss approached my work station and said, "Natalie, did you just visit a woman and talk to her son about an assault by a teacher at school?" Of course I responded, "Yes, sir." "And Natalie, did you tell the woman that she needed to sort out her dirty fish tank as you left? Because I've just had her on the phone for twenty minutes complaining about the Child Protection Police dealing with matters of animal welfare. Maybe next time you should forget about the fish?" I replied, "Okay, yes sir, but the tank was really very dirty," as everyone in the office exploded with laughter.

# CHAPTER TWENTY-TWO

# Historic Child Sexual Abuse Specialist?

Whilst working for CPT I developed a strong interest in historic cases of child sexual abuse. I suppose it makes sense as I had always been interested in "cold cases" and "unsolved murders" and these cases were similar in many ways. They required proper detective work to fit all of the pieces together, tracing witnesses from the past and bringing things to light that had lain dormant, sometimes for decades. It was also very rewarding work as I played a part in finally getting justice for the victims who had remained silent for so long. Most officers developed an area of special interest during their police service and this was definitely mine.

The most rewarding result I had was on a case I worked on alone for a year. A man in his forties contacted police stating that he had been subjected to sexual abuse for a two year period whilst he was at a reform school over thirty years before. He named the suspect as one of his teachers who was now working as a church warden having also been a social worker in the past. The suspect was previously of good character as far as I could tell and I knew that we might have trouble proving the case. I decided to search for other potential victims to try to bolster the case against the suspect. It was imperative when doing this that I didn't give out information about the suspect as I knew that in a court case later down the line a defence barrister might suggest that I had planted allegations of abuse in the minds of any additional victims as I was the one who had contacted them.

There were a few active leads to follow. Amongst some old social services paperwork I found a previous allegation against the subject when he had been a senior social worker in the 1980s. The allegation was made by a boy in the care system at the time. When the allegation was investigated, the boy changed his mind and, unfortunately, the social worker accepted this, believing there was evidence the boy had fabricated the story; she described the victim as "manipulative". I was saddened to read of this missed opportunity but carried out some research on this potential victim. Unfortunately, he was in prison for an unrelated matter so I arranged to visit him.

At the prison I simply said, "I know that you made an allegation against someone in the past and that you later withdrew it. I just want to know whether what you originally said was true because I am re-investigating the matter due to new information." The man bravely confirmed that the allegation had been true and that the suspect had persuaded him to drop the allegation at the time. He was now willing to give a statement and give evidence in court. It helped the case that this man didn't know and had never met the first victim. I also traced the original social worker who remembered the allegation being made.

I then decided to try to trace teachers and pupils who had been at the reform school thirty years before. The school itself had closed down prior to this investigation, around the 1990s, so this was a tough task. The original victim had given me a list of names including those with whom he shared a dormitory and so this was where I started.

As a long shot I searched the National Voters Register and tried to narrow down the list of likely people from the school. I contacted another police force and asked them to check an address in their area for one of the names I had found. I couldn't quite believe it when they phoned me back later with a phone number for the man who confirmed that he had been at the school and had shared a room with the victim. When I phoned him I simply said that I was investigating an allegation and that I needed to know if anything had happened at the school that had worried or concerned him. After a moment's hesitation he named my suspect and told me that he had also been sexually assaulted by him. He gave specific details and said he had informed a teacher at the school at the time; he named the teacher. The incident had had a huge impact on him and affected him into adulthood, and he was ready to go to court.

Even more incredibly, after this I managed to trace the teacher who had allegedly been informed of the assault. I asked him whether he had ever been told anything by a pupil that worried or concerned him as I had received an allegation. He immediately knew what I was talking about, naming the child and the teacher. He said that he had taken the allegation to the headmaster but that he didn't know what the outcome had been. The headmaster had died a long time ago. This teacher was also willing to give evidence in court.

I tried to trace some of the other boys without success and then I met one man who had been at the school but was now suffering from extreme mental health issues. With cases like these there has to be a cut-off point or they can go on forever. I found it difficult to accept this as I wanted to dot all the i's and cross the t's by tracing every boy and all of the teachers at the school, but I had to accept that wasn't feasible and actually what I had gathered already was very strong evidence against the suspect.

The suspect was arrested at his home address and didn't even bother to act as if he was surprised when I told him the details; it was almost as if he had been expecting it for some time. I felt desperately sorry for his wife who obviously knew nothing about any of this throughout the proceedings. Due to the overwhelming evidence against the suspect, he was later charged.

This was to be a big case for me as a junior detective and my first court case in CPT. I knew that I owed it to the victims to get things right and the burden weighed heavily on me as the officer in charge of the case. Then I was informed that the suspect was being represented by a prominent barrister, of whom the rest of my office were afraid. I heard stories of officers being forced to recite huge sections of our operating manual (Police and Criminal Evidence Act, PACE) in the witness box and of one senior officer being reduced to tears whilst giving evidence. I tried not to listen to these rumours but couldn't help but be nervous.

I was somewhat in awe of judges in general and had a healthy fear of the legal power they held at their fingertips. I was aware of a case locally where either a journalist or solicitor had been sentenced for contempt of court and spent a day on the wrong side of the door of a court cell because her phone had gone off one too many times. To be fair to the judge, in this particular case there had been fair warning given but this type of thing definitely put the rest of us on high alert during all court proceedings.

I didn't know anything about the trial judge who was to be presiding over my case but he was considered "kind" by other officers. I wasn't sure if this meant "kind" to victims, suspects, or police officers so it didn't reassure me. The judge with the most fearsome reputation at that time was Judge Brown, whom officers referred to as "Send-'em-down Brown" either because of how he addressed the defendants before he sent them to prison or due to the numbers of defendants he sent to prison in the first place.

I had appeared in court many times since my probationary blunder with the drink driver and the only slight mishap since then occurred when I was asked to quote the police caution, which I had done perfectly apart from the last line which I missed out completely due to nerves. On that occasion, after a lengthy pause with all eyes on me, the barrister helpfully added, "And did you also say that anything they did say could be used in evidence?" as I gratefully smiled at the hasty rescue and confirmed that "yes, of course" I had said that as well.

The day arrived and all of the witnesses turned up, which is usually the first hurdle. It was a bit awkward as we had to try to keep the witnesses separated and as a witness myself I couldn't speak to any of them about the case. I found this difficult as I didn't want them to think I didn't care about them or was detaching myself for a petty reason so I asked the prosecution barrister to explain my position to them.

All of the victims and witnesses bravely testified as planned and the trial seemed to be going well. One especially emotional moment occurred when the second man from the reform school gave his evidence from behind a screen to shield his face from the suspect as he couldn't bear to see him. He broke down in tears with the recollection. I struggled to contain my own emotion as this broken man told his story. Later when the suspect gave his evidence and denied everything, I just kept thinking, "Why would a grown man travel all of this way to tell a story about something that didn't happen to him thirty years ago and then break down in the witness box?"

One of the highlights of the trial was when the defence barrister suggested to several of the witnesses that I had given them the name of the suspect I was investigating. All of the witnesses said that I hadn't done this and that I had explained to them that it could jeopardise any later court case. At this the judge commented "Yes, the officer was right." I was still worried about giving evidence, though, anticipating hours in the witness box going over and over details. However, in the end the prosecution barrister had an informal chat with the defence barrister to establish what his intentions were in relation to me and whilst I was present in the room he helpfully replied, "Don't worry, I'm not going after her," as I breathed a sigh of relief. I knew that this meant that I had done a good job with the investigation and didn't need to worry about any surprises.

It's important to understand the role of a judge in a case like this. The judge oversees the case and makes decisions about points of law but the jury decides on points of fact. The judge should be impartial and mustn't lead the jury one way or the other regarding a verdict or the case could later be lost if there is an appeal. One of my favourite moments in a court case is after the jury have delivered their verdict and the judge is finally able to speak freely about the case as they no longer have to worry about improperly influencing the jury. During their speech they make it clear how they feel about the suspect and the crime that has been committed and their comments are often profound.

My case was no exception and the "kind" judge vanished as the jury delivered their guilty verdict and he let out all of the things he had no doubt been desperate to express as the case progressed. He focused on the fact that by choosing to plead "not guilty" the suspect had forced the victims to endure the indignation and humiliation of a court trial in the media spotlight in addition to the original abuse. He made it clear that he believed the jury had delivered the correct verdict and that he would not be granting the suspect bail as he would be receiving a lengthy prison sentence.

I was lost in a whirlwind of silent emotion from the point when I heard the jury read the "guilty" verdicts to the court. I had invested so much in this case emotionally and had become caught up in the lives of the victims. I wasn't prepared when the judge addressed me directly by name. He commented that he wasn't going to ask me to stand as he could see the effect the case had had on me; I was shaking. He said that I was most highly commended for my work on the case and that the victims and wider society owed me a debt of gratitude. He said that he would be sending a copy of his comments to my supervisors. This was probably the proudest moment of my career and made all of the hard work worthwhile. Then he looked at the suspect with contempt as he uttered the words, "Take him down," to the prison officers who had appeared next to the suspect in the dock when he was found guilty.

The judge later sentenced the suspect to fourteen years in prison for his crimes, a sentence that even I had not been expecting due to the historic nature of the offences and the age of the suspect, who was also in poor health. I was awarded a Certificate of Merit for my work on the case at a special awards ceremony.

# CHAPTER TWENTY-THREE

# The Turning Point

Socially, throughout this period, I continued living a worldly lifestyle, but was becoming more and more miserable. In my heart I knew that I could never be 100% happy without God. I knew He was there and that I couldn't continue to ignore Him forever. It was at the beginning of 2005 that I was really getting to the end of my tether. I was desperately pursuing happiness in worldly things, often to extremes, but finding no satisfaction, fulfilment, purpose, or meaning in my life. Eventually, after six years of this lifestyle, I reached the end of my own resources; I realised that enough was enough. I asked God for forgiveness for my many sins and was determined to live a new life before Him. I started changing things straight away. I stopped drinking, smoking and gambling and went back to church. I had learnt the meaninglessness and hopelessness of life without God and didn't ever want to experience it again.

My dramatic re-commitment to Christianity caused a big stir at work as my colleagues immediately noticed the drastic change in my life. Soon after this, I was driving to work one day and obviously wasn't paying enough attention; as I went over a small hill, I suddenly found a long queue of traffic at a standstill in front of me. It was a main road and I was travelling too fast to stop in time. I knew I would hit the rear vehicle so I automatically swerved around and to the side of it, thinking that I might be able to travel down the side of the queue. Fortunately, there was nothing in the lane I swerved into as this would have been a high impact collision, but I did hit the rear corner of the last car in the queue. This impact shunted me across the road and into the path of an HGV in the inside lane which almost managed to stop in time and just shunted my car slightly along the road. I heard the sound of crashing glass and found myself surrounded by people trying to help. I was not injured but was obviously shaken and the passenger side of my vehicle was staved in. (This was my second serious collision and vehicle write-off as in 2001, whilst driving my brand new car to work, I had skidded on black ice and hit a tree, miraculously escaping unharmed.)

I decided after this that I didn't want to get another car for a while. I therefore travelled on the train to and from work for about six months which resulted in an interesting encounter. I was standing on the train heading home from work when I saw a group of rough looking youngsters (or maybe gangsters would be more accurate). They were drinking, smoking and swearing, and most people avoided them as they made their presence known. I saw that one of them had the word "HATE" tattooed across his knuckles. For some reason seeing this made me feel sad and I wanted to reach out to them in some way but I knew it would be dangerous as I was alone. So I prayed silently that I would get an opportunity to talk to them, half thinking that it was a crazy prayer but believing it was possible. When I reached my home station, the guys ran off the train ahead of me; they ran through the underpass shouting abuse and dodging the security guard who shouted after them as they obviously didn't have tickets for the train. One of them stuck his middle finger up at the CCTV camera as he ran. I followed at a distance through the underpass thinking that my opportunity had passed.

Unbelievably, as I neared the underpass exit, one of the guys stopped, turned back and then approached me saying, "We weren't too bad, were we?" I was in total shock but felt compelled and duty bound to say, "Well you really should have paid for your tickets and I am a police officer!" This guy then fell into step next to me and as we left the station, one of the other guys joined us. I couldn't believe that they had slowed down to talk to me as they could easily have been caught by the security guards at this point. Instead of being intimidated or angered when I identified myself as a "cop", they were fascinated and began bombarding me with questions about my job.

Sensing my opportunity I turned to the guy with the tattooed hands and said, "You're not happy are you?" He ignored this but I repeated it and then he said, "No, I'm not, actually." I responded "Well, you know what would make you happy; you should go to church and learn about God." He didn't react as I was expecting but seemed interested and said, "Really, are you a Christian, then? I might just do that!" I confirmed that I *was* a Christian and the three of us then talked about our lifestyles. I was able to share parts of my testimony and tell them about my church. The one with the hate tattoo then gave me a hug and said to me, "Natalie, you took the time out to speak to us. If I see you again, we will sit down and have a chat." They then pointed out their house to me and walked off. I was left in a bit of a daze.

Later at work (and with permission from my supervisor) I carried out some research and identified the young man I had been talking to as a well-known local criminal. He was listed as a dangerous psychopath with an intense hatred of the police, and on his previous arrests, they had required at least eight officers to restrain him! Now he was living near to me and considered himself to be an acquaintance of mine! Over time incidents like this made me realise that my faith might conflict with my role as a police officer. I wanted to help these people as I had compassion for them but sometimes I felt my hands were tied due to my job and the necessity to remain impartial.

# CHAPTER TWENTY-FOUR

# Professional Standards Department (PSD)

The most hated and feared department in Sussex Police? Probably the Professional Standards Department. PSD is another name for "Internal Investigations". The job: to root out and get rid of corrupt officers. Unfortunately, over time they had built up a reputation across the force for pursuing not only the bad eggs but also the hard working and honest officers who happened to make the odd mistake. Everybody knew who the PSD officers were and the minute one of them entered a building, the whisper would start, "PSD are in the building," followed by the obvious question, "Who are they here for?"

I actually liked the idea of working in PSD but knew it wasn't a possibility for some time as they were only staffed with inspectors or above. I had been on a course with one of these inspectors and found out all about the role, and determined that this was a goal for the future. However, I didn't need to wait long as the department suddenly opened its doors to detective constables and held an application procedure shortly afterwards. I didn't hold out much hope as I was still young and in competition with experienced officers across the force.

At first I was also a bit reluctant to leave Child Protection as I was still enjoying the work. However, when I dealt with three incidents of a particularly distressing nature within a few days, it made me realise it was time to move on. I am not going to go into too much detail but one of the cases involved the accidental death of a seven-year-old child. I reluctantly fulfilled my obligation by attending the scene of the incident, all the way there dreading seeing the body of the poor child, only to find, to my relief, that the body had already been removed. This was too close for comfort for me as I knew that had I seen something like this, it would have stayed with me for the rest of my life.

The other two cases involved the sexual abuse of children and one of these cases affected me deeply. Whilst interviewing the suspect I realised that I was dealing with a level of depravity that I hadn't known existed and I wasn't adequately prepared for it. Historic child abuse was one thing as those children were now adults and although the abuse they had suffered was terrible and sometimes they had suffered silently for many years, I hadn't had to witness the suffering first hand and was able to assist them in obtaining the justice they deserved. Current child abuse was something else, hearing young children describing details of abuse in an innocent and matter-of-fact manner, having no idea why these things have been happening or what the perpetrator is really doing to them, really sickened me and I knew that enough was enough.

I was surprised to pass the PSD interview and to be offered a job to begin in February 2006. During the selection procedure some interesting things emerged. I was asked a lot of questions about the flat that I had moved into in 2004. The flat had been owned by my parents for a number of years. I was asked about my association with the previous tenant of the flat and whether I had ever met him, etc. I said that I hadn't but then suddenly remembered that my dad had introduced me to him on one occasion when he was showing me around the flat before I moved in. I was stood in the living room in front of the large window facing out onto the street and had shaken his hand. I wondered what on earth all this was about.

I was informed that the previous tenant was heavily involved in criminal activity. I was astonished but suddenly things began to fall into place. The guy had suddenly needed to move out, giving little notice and stating he was going away somewhere for a few months; prison as it turned out. There was also a round indentation mark near the lock on the outside of my flat door which I now recognised as a previous forced entry by the police. I made sure the records were updated but found it quite amusing that my dad hadn't realised what was going on as there is no way he would have allowed this guy to move in had he realised. But there we were shaking hands amiably in the front room with my dad telling me what a nice guy and reliable tenant this man was, completely oblivious to the fact that we were probably under police surveillance and now listed as associates of this local drug baron!

Living in this flat created more than enough drama to match my duties at work as the couple on the floor above me had frequent domestic rows which turned violent and I often had to call the police to come and deal with the situation. It was then that I realised how dangerous our domestic violence policies were as even though I had heard the couple threatening to kill each other, screaming in pain and hurling objects around, very little was done by the police who attended. I assume this was because the couple lied to protect each other on police arrival, as is the case in so many domestic incidents. Occasionally one or other of them was arrested; I overheard a mention of a stiletto heel being used as a weapon on one such occasion. I was petrified that they would end up killing each other and was always relieved when one of them moved out for some respite.

Anyway, life in PSD was not as exciting as I had hoped. I can't give details of many of my cases for obvious reasons but I spent most of my time trying to re-educate officers who were under investigation about the role of PSD. I tried to help them to see that PSD was working to uncover the truth and that they only needed to worry if they had deliberately done something wrong. I had some success, particularly at stations I had recently worked at, as people knew me as one of them and didn't yet see me as part of the PSD machine.

What I was telling them was true: my observation was that PSD was only working to root out corruption and not to take down innocent officers for mistakes. During my time in the department I saw no evidence of PSD pursuing honest officers for simple mistakes. If an officer made an honest mistake, the investigation was thorough, but the purpose was to protect the officer from further investigation, which could occur if they didn't investigate properly in the first place or if the police watchdog (IPCC) investigated later.

Sussex Police had its fair share of shocking moments where prominent senior officers disgraced themselves, but generally other officers were ashamed when this happened. I was particularly saddened by several of these incidents as even when I didn't know the officers well, I still knew of them and in some cases had worked alongside or been supervised by them. The important thing to remember is that even though they may have gained a high rank they were still humans facing the same temptations and struggles in life that we all face, and sometimes they fell. There were also a number of suicides across the force, which were truly devastating for families and loved ones and affected every officer to one degree or another.

Another regular occurrence which sent ripples of shock through the force was the "retired officer death" emails that we were sent. We checked the ages of these people and found that they were often in their fifties. Actually the average life expectancy of a police officer after they retire is just seven years. In my case, if I had completed my service, that would have been just fifty-six as I started young. I think the combination of stress, shift work and living an unhealthy lifestyle due to shift work are to blame for these shocking statistics.

PSD deal with complaints from members of the public as well as internal complaints. One procedure which was misunderstood across the force was called "local resolution". Used correctly this was really a great idea but, unfortunately, officers were so afraid and distrusting of PSD that the procedure often failed. The idea was based on the assumption that when most members of the public complain, what they really want is an honest explanation and maybe an apology from the officer involved. However, most officers are reluctant to do this as they fear the consequences of admitting guilt and that they may be disciplined or even sacked. If a member of the public agrees to a local resolution of their complaint, it means that they cannot later pursue formal sanctions against the officer, effectively making the officer free to speak without fear of consequence. Obviously they cannot admit criminal activity or dishonesty, but they should be free to admit honest mistakes.

However, most officers didn't trust the system, which resulted in some ridiculous situations. A PSD officer spent hours listening sympathetically to and then talking to a complainant. They tried to persuade the complainant that they were more likely to find out what had happened and possibly receive an apology if they agreed to a local resolution. The complainant often agreed to this based on the recommendation of the PSD officer. However, when the PSD officer approached the officer to obtain their explanation or response, the officer often responded with, "no comment," believing that they would get in trouble if they gave an explanation. This was a totally inappropriate response to deliver to the already upset person who had complained. I spent a lot of time trying to help officers understand this procedure so that they would feel able to give a proper response to the complainant.

One case on which I worked was reported not only in the local press but in national and world news. It was a mass sweet theft or, as the headlines put it, "Cops Rapped in Lolly Theft". One police station began experiencing thefts from their tuck shop and had set up CCTV equipment to monitor what was going on. This turned into a highly entertaining investigation as we witnessed one officer making a bed out of some chairs and going to sleep for half of his night shift (which had to be dealt with as a separate issue) and a cleaning lady inadvertently swapping the plugs for the fridge and the CCTV thus temporarily disabling the camera! One officer also poked a pen right into the lens of the camera convincing us that he must be aware of its existence due to his accuracy. There were so many questions raised by the CCTV footage that we had to interview nearly everybody who used the tuck shop, resulting in sixteen officers being temporarily removed from front line duties. This was a massive problem for a small station as it was nearly half of the officers! In the end the officers were given advice about making sure they paid for items at the time of purchase rather than keeping running tallies of money owed in their heads, as tuck shops were rapidly banned across the force to prevent a similar embarrassment in the future. Reflecting on the case, I am convinced that most officers involved were honest and that it wasn't a case of an entire station of corruption, just a faulty accounting procedure.

After just six months in PSD I had had enough. The department was in a state of transition when I arrived as they had not previously been staffed by junior detectives and I found that I didn't have enough work to do most of the time. I wanted to be busy and was frustrated by the slower pace of life in the department which suited other officers nearing the end of their careers. I suppose it's a good sign that the department didn't have high workloads and reflects well on the force as a whole, but it just didn't work for me at that stage of my career. A transfer was arranged for me on request. I was returned to CID at a completely new station: Shoreham.

## CHAPTER TWENTY-FIVE

# Sleepy Shoreham, a Cannabis Café and a Brothel!

After the initial suspicions that I was a PSD spy sent to gather and capture intelligence died down, I threw myself wholeheartedly into the CID role at Shoreham as I had missed the active duty having held an office job for a while. To start with I shocked some of the uniformed officers by enthusiastically getting involved in some low level crime investigations and attending non-CID incidents. Detectives are only required to attend and investigate the more serious criminal offences such as burglary, robbery and rape, but part of our role was also to support the uniformed officers when they were busy. We would also investigate bulk and series crime which often began its life with some poor response officer who clearly didn't have enough time to investigate it thoroughly whilst responding to emergencies on a daily basis.

I attended one such incident in order to assist a uniformed officer in viewing the contents of a large container lorry or truck which may have been linked to serious crime. On arrival, we discovered that the container was completely full of used tyres. The item we were searching for was quite small. It would be necessary to remove all of the tyres to search it properly. The uniformed officer looked at me, no doubt expecting me to offer my excuses as I slunk back to the police station wondering why I had volunteered to attend in the first place. This may have been the sensible thing to do as I was wearing a smart suit and black shoes. Throwing caution to the wind, I jumped into the back of the container and began the slow process of lifting the tyres and rolling them towards my colleague at the back, in the process shocking both him and the manager of the breaker's yard where the vehicle was stowed. Unfortunately, we didn't find what we were looking for. News quickly travels in police stations, and for a few days afterwards I was the female detective who "got her suit dirty removing tyres from the back of a lorry"!

The most unusual case at Shoreham made global headlines as a man had allegedly been running a large brothel in a middle-class neighbourhood undetected. The residents were understandably up in arms about this outrage in their community and on attending the house I was appalled at the living conditions and the many unsightly and unsanitary items found within. In the end, after attempting to pursue the matter criminally and failing drastically, we dealt with the situation by working with the local council to move the man on as he had taken out a huge mortgage on the property that he couldn't afford and was heavily in debt. We called it "The Ways and Means Act". It suited us and the residents who could now return to their pleasant neighbourhood strolls without the indignity of scantily clad women and gangs of men arriving accidentally on their doorsteps when they went to the wrong house.

The biggest news at Shoreham at this time was, as local residents will definitely remember, "The Cannabis Café" that was frequently opened, shut down and then re-opened in Lancing. The organisers were well versed in the relevant aspects of the law and very determined in their efforts to keep the place open despite the obviously illegal activity occurring within. One inspector at Shoreham made it his personal goal to take down this place which was so blatantly operating on his patch. In the end he hired a huge bulldozer to tear down the entrance gates as a specialist team stormed in to gather the dregs of the drug paraphernalia. Unfortunately (or fortunately, depending on your perspective), this action made the building unstable, so no one was allowed in for a while. I am unsure of the eventual outcome but it gave the local media a good story and I was definitely impressed by the diligence of our inspector and the creativity of his methods.

As it was so difficult to find evidence of actual drugs, the main perpetrator and organiser of the café was constantly arrested for other offences that he was committing in order to make him aware that the criminal activity would not be tolerated. He was considered dangerous, being heavily built and not afraid to use his muscle as he had demonstrated on numerous occasions. I arrested him once and found him extremely compliant (maybe because I am female) in contrast to the many violent fighting arrests that took place when between six and eight male officers tried to take him into custody. In the end, I think he moved on and opened another "café" elsewhere.

One particularly despicable crime that was very hard to solve was that of the artifice burglar. These were the people who turned up on the doorsteps of elderly people pretending to be from the water board or the bank. On this basis they were usually then invited into the house and proceeded to steal whatever they could lay their hands on, which sometimes turned out to be the person's life savings which had been safely stowed under a mattress.

Unfortunately, these criminals often operated in groups and swapped clothing and vehicles amongst themselves. The only way to catch them was in the act of committing the crime, but usually the victim was so traumatised when they realised what had happened that they called a relative rather than the police, or they didn't realise what had happened until much later by which point the opportunity had been lost. We had an e-fit developed for one of our series of crimes (basically a sketch of what the suspect looks like based on witness accounts) and I recognised one of our local villains who had previous involvement in similar crimes, so we arrested him. Our plan was to place him on an identification procedure with the witnesses and ask them to identify him. This was really clutching at straws as the victims were elderly people with poor eyesight and some had problems with their memory or mental health issues, which is sadly the reason they had been targeted in the first place.

When the suspect came into custody to be interviewed, even I didn't recognise him as he had changed his appearance to the extent that he looked like a completely different person. The problem for us was that the law only allows us to tell the person that they shouldn't change their appearance between the time of arrest and their filming for (or attendance at) an identification procedure, but this guy had changed it after committing the crime and before being arrested. Obviously we couldn't prove that he had done this because of the type of crimes he was committing, but it was such a blatant change that I thought it must be able to be used to build a case against him in some way. It was just circumstantial evidence and we would need a lot more than that to charge him.

I looked back over his previous arrests and saw that every time he had been into custody he looked drastically different, with different hair colour, style, facial hair, and even facial expressions. He was obviously a con artist but acted as if he didn't have a clue what was going on whilst he was in police custody, as if the whole procedure was new to him. This particular guy also had a brother who looked very like him, which complicated everything as they often used each other's names and other details. In the end the arrested suspect wasn't identified by any of our witnesses and one witness even chose someone else who had nothing to do with the matter, so we had to let our suspect go. Sometimes we were dealing with a set of impossible circumstances working against us but I believed these people would eventually get caught. To be honest, I sometimes wondered how non-Christian officers dealt with some of the injustices and failed court cases. At least, as a Christian, I knew that if we didn't catch them they weren't getting away with it forever as they would face the judgement of God one day for their crimes.

One of the aspects of working as a detective that I enjoyed the most was working night shifts and being the only detective on duty for the whole area (which was huge). I hadn't enjoyed working regular night shifts as part of a pattern on uniform but in CID it was different as we were on an annual rotation and worked seven nights in a row about twice a year. As I was seeking evidence that I would be competent to operate at the next rank as a sergeant, the night shifts were a great opportunity to make decisions and manage crime scenes. I even volunteered to do an extra set at short notice to cover for someone else. Of course, there were detective supervisors on call and we had the support of the uniformed supervision, but I always enjoyed the extra responsibility and the chance to learn.

A typical night shift might involve dealing with one rape allegation or a house burglary or, more likely (especially at the weekend), a serious assault. The problem came when the serious incidents occurred all at the same time and in different areas of the division. I recall one night early in my shift dealing with an allegation of drug dealing in Shoreham, then being contacted about an arson with suspects in custody at Worthing. Whilst dealing with that I received a call to advise me that there had been a serious domestic assault in Littlehampton, and a few hours later a dead body had been found in the street at Chichester. Obviously I had to prioritise the Chichester matter and began the long drive towards Chichester having contacted the on-call detective sergeant (DS). Half-way there I received another call advising that five people had been arrested in Shoreham for a suspected grievous bodily harm assault. I pulled my car over wondering what on earth to do, before contacting the DS again to advise that I wasn't going to make it to Chichester and was heading back to Shoreham. This type of craziness was, fortunately, rare and it was still a good opportunity to learn to prioritise incidents, to manage things and to give advice from a distance without always being present at the scene.

Being the duty detective on nights and the fact that I was still relatively inexperienced due to the time I had spent in other departments, I inevitably made mistakes, sometimes major ones. The biggest mistake I recall, which was later recovered by my supervisor, occurred when I attended an allegation of a possible "drink spiking" incident. The woman wasn't alleging that anything untoward had happened to her after she believed her drink may have been spiked, but she seemed confused. I obtained details from her and carried out some basic investigations, then arranged for her to go to a friend's house for the rest of the night.

On night shifts the general rule was that if we could secure evidence to allow a better investigation in daylight hours, then that is what we would do. My mistake in this case was that I hadn't checked whether there was any of the "spiked drink" left or taken the glasses that had been used for forensic testing; quite an obvious part of the investigation and a foolish oversight on my part. Luckily, the detectives who attended the next day found the half-consumed glasses and bottle exactly as they had been when I had attended. Tests were conducted on the fluid and there was no evidence of a foreign substance present, but if there had been, I might have been in trouble.

# CHAPTER TWENTY-SIX

# Wasting Police Time

In 2006 the now notorious book "Wasting Police Time"[2] by the mysterious (and later revealed to be fictitious) "PC David Copperfield" was published. Every police officer (including me) got hold of a copy and read it avidly as politicians and senior officers fought to be the first to condemn and contradict the bold assertions in the book. Sadly, the reason the book created such a stir and was so popular amongst rank and file officers was because the stories were essentially true and representative of the experiences of officers across the nation. At last we had a public voice for the craziness that had been developing over a number of years within the national police service due to the badly planned and executed experiments of the government of the day. For quite some time officers had been remarking to each other, "If only the public knew about this." Those who did dare to speak out usually did so loudly and tactlessly so it was easy for them to be swiftly dealt with and later, if they continued with their crusade, to be dispensed with for insubordination.

For many years we were encouraged to write our reports to say what adhered to what the government wanted the statistics to show (although this was never officially acknowledged): less violent crime, fewer sexual offences, fewer burglaries, etc. This was an art in itself as the trick was to state what you knew the higher powers wanted to hear

---

[2] Published by Monday Books (2006); ISBN 9780955285417

without actually lying. At first I challenged the system, along with other officers, believing that what we were doing was wrong, but our protests fell on deaf ears. Our reports kept getting sent back for "updating and further investigation" which became tedious and over time we fell in line. The change in requirements was subtle and happened gradually over a few years, resulting in many officers forgetting that they were manipulating statistics and beginning to see this as a normal way to carry on.

One of the products of this era was the new and very lengthy stop forms[3] that we were required to complete every time we spoke to anyone. It was no longer possible to carry these in our pocket books when we were actually talking to the person on the street as they were now three times the size. The strangest part of the form, which I'm sure I can put down to political correctness, was the "self-defined ethnicity section". Officers were first required to define the person's ethnicity by choosing from six options, which was a fairly standard practice dating back some years. But now, in addition, the person being spoken to was required to define their own ethnicity and there were not six but sixteen options. This had people, who were no doubt already embarrassed at having been stopped in the street by the police, scratching their heads and looking bewildered as they tried to work out whether they were Afro-Caribbean or Mixed Caribbean or one of the other mildly different options.

My wakeup call came a few years down the line when I had been promoted to sergeant and a new officer joined my team. This officer submitted some reports which I knew would be sent back from senior officers and I found myself explaining how the reports should be worded in order to get them filed. The officer's reply was that what I was suggesting wasn't what had actually happened and that they didn't want to lie in the report. I explained that it wasn't lying but just the way the report should be written, but this really pricked my conscience. I wish the force had withstood government pressure, as I began to resent being put in that position, especially as a Christian.

At the worst point of this absurdity we were instructed to record every crime, even those with no identifiable victim or suspect. If a

---

[3] A 'stop form' contains basic personal details and the circumstances of a stop along with the officer's name and badge number.

victim didn't want to prosecute a suspect, we were still forced to generate mountains of paperwork and interview the suspect for something called "Home Office Statistics". We criminalised children who had had minor quarrels with their friends, interviewing them and issuing reprimands or cautions. All of our discretion was removed and we had no power to make common sense decisions. If we tried to make our own decisions, maybe for the benefit of all persons involved in a crime, the files came bouncing back from senior officers requiring re-investigation. We were basically turned into robots following ever increasing numbers of rules and regulations which had obviously not been written by people who had any idea about day-to-day policing. Morale hit rock bottom and many officers left the police force due to sheer frustration.

The new system continued for quite a while even after the "Wasting Police Time" book was published, although some minor changes were made in response to the public outcry. Most people believed that the allegations made in the book couldn't possibly be true, although if they had really looked into the matter they would have found clear evidence that they were. One major clue was the lack of civil libel and defamation suits following the publication. In actual fact when a politician boldly stated that the book was a pack of lies, using parliamentary privilege, the publisher responded by stating that they would sue the politician if he cared to repeat his comments in public!

# CHAPTER TWENTY-SEVEN

# Priority Crime Team

For a few months I was assigned to a Worthing unit called the "Priority Crime Team" which, unbeknownst to me, was basically a product of the statistic manipulation era. The role of the department was to target suspects who were already in police custody or in prison and try to clear up or obtain confessions for unsolved prior crimes. If the suspect admits the crimes, these unresolved offences are said to be "taken into consideration" (TIC). Usually if a suspect admits TICs in addition to the crimes they are charged with, they will not receive much of an additional sentence at court. The idea is that they can confess all of their crimes in one hit so that they will not be re-arrested for prior crimes on their release from prison.

Sometimes we took prisoners out of prison and drove round with them in plain cars so that they could point out locations of their prior crimes. The drive around was an attempt to jog their memories, but we also had to build relationships with the prisoners to encourage them to be open with us. We then compared their admissions with reports of crime and often found that crimes hadn't been reported or the owners were not aware that there had even been a crime. One of the more amusing stories I recall was one prisoner who admitted regularly stealing meat from a freezer in a shed in a back garden. There had been no reports of theft and when we spoke to the owner, she told us that she had been blaming her husband for eating the meat and it had caused several domestic rows!

As we drove past one road, this same prisoner began talking about breaking into a vehicle with some other people, stealing the CD player and running off down the road. He said that as they turned the corner within thirty seconds of the break-in, they heard police sirens and were stopped by a police patrol car. They had just managed to hide the stolen items behind a nearby fence and make it appear as if they were walking along the road, not running. The prisoner had also been wanted on a court warrant at the time of the stop. As he was talking I started thinking that this story seemed vaguely familiar. He said that the police asked for their names and he had given a false name. The police asked them if they had seen anyone running and so they pointed in another direction and sent the police after another group of boys.

With shock I suddenly realised that I had been in the police car that had stopped this guy. I thought back to the incident and remembered that he had been with some high profile criminals from the area and that they were just a few hundred metres from the break-in when we stopped them. I also remembered that I had been aware that this guy was wanted at the time that we had stopped him but hadn't recognised him. We had been in such a rush to find the suspects that we had failed to see the elephant in the room: the guys we had stopped were the offenders. I was embarrassed to recall that we hadn't searched them or even recorded their details. We had just asked for their names, asked for ID which they said they didn't have and then sped off. Normally, I was very thorough with this type of thing and would even make a suspect give me a phone number to call to confirm their identity, which usually resolved any lies regarding personal details. As soon as someone said that there was no one I could call, I knew they were lying! The guy said that they had returned later and collected the stolen items. This was a humiliating moment for me as we should have known these guys were responsible or have at least searched them thoroughly and checked their ID.

After a few weeks I began to feel uncomfortable about the nature of the work I was doing in this unit, and again I wondered how the public would feel if they knew how their money was being spent. Taking the prisoners out for the day, hoping that they would admit prior crimes which would then be added to their case at court (with the possibility that they wouldn't receive an additional sentence) all for the ultimate purpose of government statistics. Trying to sell this to victims also became hard as there was no easy way for them to obtain any form of compensation when a case was dealt with like this. I felt as if I were deceiving people and the way that we had to build relationships with these criminals also felt wrong. I requested a transfer pretty quickly and went back to CID.

However, time in this department also made me realise that I would never be in a position to help a person spiritually whilst in the police. Dealing with prisoners (actually in prisons rather than just in temporary police custody) and building relationships with them allowed me to see up close the hopelessness and meaningless of many of their lives and I wanted desperately to help them in a deeper way by sharing my faith with them. I knew I couldn't do this openly; it would be seen as "wrong" in the eyes of senior police officers as it is not politically correct and someone might be offended. There have been recent examples of this in other professions; the doctor who offered to pray for a patient and was later sacked after thirty years in his profession, for example.

Sometimes if people were really interested, I did tell prisoners of my own personal experiences and encouraged them to seek God for themselves, but that was the extent to which I felt able to go. Of course, I was able to share openly with colleagues but when it came to people I met through my work as a police officer, it was different. I did meet a prisoner on one occasion who was really desperate to find meaning in his life. He started a conversation and we had a good discussion about faith. I encouraged him in his spiritual journey and later sent him a letter with further details and my pastor's contact information for further correspondence, but it still felt inadequate. However, there wasn't really anything I could do about this so I pushed it to the back of my mind at that time.

# CHAPTER TWENTY-EIGHT

# Temporary Promotion

After a while as a detective at Shoreham, I was approached and offered an opportunity to be a temporary detective sergeant at Worthing for three weeks to cover an absence. Of course, I said yes, and prepared myself. I was thrown in at the deep end with this role as the absent sergeant had been covering two teams, so I found myself supervising a total of seven detectives instead of the normal three or four. I ended up working late every day and experienced very high workloads but I enjoyed the challenge.

The case that stands out was that of an alleged rape of a child by a stranger. This is probably the most serious type of allegation that can be received, excluding murder. Initially my supervisor (detective inspector) was running the case, but before an arrest had been made in the case, he had to go on pre-planned leave. He left me in charge of the investigation which was a real challenge as I didn't really know what I was doing and had to improvise at every step. The offence was alleged to have taken place in a public area with an electronic swipe card entry system and membership list. The entrance also had CCTV cameras. On reviewing the investigation, I knew that the key to identifying the suspect was the CCTV and that we needed to be very thorough with this. The problem was that several times the staff reviewing the tapes came back saying they couldn't find anything. I sent them back to continue trying as I knew the suspect had to be on the CCTV and that they just needed to spend more time looking. I also thought that if we could pinpoint the suspect entering or leaving using the swipe card, we would have a name. Eventually, we obtained a name for the suspect from the CCTV and swipe card entry and planned to make an arrest.

Fortunately, I reminded the team that they should only make an arrest if the suspect matched the description of the man seen on the CCTV with the girl. The team later returned stating that the man they had been about to arrest didn't match the description so they hadn't arrested him. I was relieved as there had nearly been a colossal mistake of identity which could have potentially ruined an innocent man's life. I then focused the investigation on another man, who had entered the public building just after the man we had nearly arrested. Maybe the timings were slightly out. There were only two possibilities looking at the CCTV and we now knew it wasn't the first man. I arranged another arrest attempt of the second man.

At this point I was taken to one side by a fellow sergeant who asked me if I was sure I knew what I was doing and whether I was confident in authorising the arrest. I explained the situation and the sergeant asked me how closely I had checked the work done with the CCTV. I said then that I believed that at some stage I had to trust the officers who had done the work as I couldn't always review every last detail. The team located the man who, fortunately, did match the description from the CCTV and later he admitted some sexual activity in his interview although he said he believed the girl was sixteen. I was pleased with the outcome but relieved when my inspector came back from leave, as this and other cases had been a steep learning curve for me.

Also during this period I attended court for a money laundering case. There was an inspector who had a particular interest in this offence having previously worked in the department that deals with Financial Crime. However, the courts generally didn't like dealing with money laundering unless it was for a large amount of money. But this inspector insisted that every time someone was stopped, investigated or arrested for any type of acquisitive crime and had quantities of cash on them, they would also be investigated for money laundering. To his credit, he was very involved in many of these cases and led by example.

So it was that I ended up at court supervising a case involving a man who had been arrested on three separate occasions with hundreds of pounds in cash on his person and had subsequently been charged with money laundering. My job, as the officer in charge of the case, was to prove that the money could not have come from any legitimate source and that it had in fact been laundered.

The defendant in the case came across poorly when giving evidence; he even went so far as to state that he had "never broken the laws of the land" before hastily adding "in relation to money laundering". I thought those present would immediately see his mistake and realise that he had had to add to his statement to avoid perjuring himself due to his extensive criminal history. Unfortunately, he was found "not guilty" by the jury on all three counts of money laundering but he did plead "guilty" to possession of a very small quantity of drugs that had been found in his possession. In a classic moment of comedy, the judge, who with her years of experience knew exactly what was going on, set a date to sentence the defendant for drug possession with the jury still present. You can probably imagine the reaction of the jury as the defendant's lawyer stated that he wouldn't be able to appear on the stated date as he had another drug related case pending at court! Then, as if to add insult to injury, the judge asked for a list of the defendant's previous convictions to be read out so that she could make a bail decision; as already mentioned, the list was extensive.

I was pretty frustrated by the outcome as I knew we would have to give the seized money back to the defendant. But it wasn't to be, as I dutifully contacted the defendant's lawyer a while later to be informed that at the sentencing hearing for the very small quantity of drugs, the judge had fined the defendant the exact amount that he was alleged to have laundered, some £800! This made the whole fiasco worthwhile and confirmed my long held opinion that judges were totally awesome. Unfortunately, it also encouraged our inspector to continue his relentless pursuit of the county's more minor money launderers at every opportunity.

# CHAPTER TWENTY-NINE

# Back to Uniform

I had now been in plain clothed detective work in some form or another for four years and saw this as my future career path. I was hoping to be offered promotion within CID at some point, maybe after some more shadowing and acting in the role, but the opportunities were limited. I was then approached by a uniformed inspector asking if I would consider returning to uniform as a sergeant at Shoreham for six months to cover a vacancy. I immediately said no, arguing that it wasn't my career path and that I had been out of uniform for so long that I wouldn't have a clue what I was doing back in that role, let alone supervising other officers. He gently encouraged me, reminding me that when I had arrived at Shoreham CID, I had said the same thing to him about that role, having been out of CID for a few years. He said that he would like me to think about it. I agreed.

So, in January 2007 I began a period of acting as a sergeant at Shoreham and I really enjoyed it. Some members of the public did show some disbelief that I was a sergeant due to my age, even though there were many other sergeants of a similar age. Mostly when people asked me how long I had been a police officer, I learnt to say, "Long enough," which usually stopped further questions. One man refused to allow me to deal with the crime he was reporting because he said I had no experience and he wanted a "proper" police officer to deal with his incident. I informed him that police officers didn't grow on trees and it was me or no one, at which point he began to cooperate.

During my first few shifts as a supervisor, one of my staff somehow managed to lose control of his handcuffs when he was halfway through cuffing a prisoner. The prisoner took possession of the cuffs and began waving them around wildly as a weapon until he was brought back under control by additional officers. In another incident shortly after this, I was negotiating with a mad man threatening to throw a pair of shears at some of my officers as he stood hanging out of a second floor window brandishing them and we stood on the grass outside. I was grateful that most of these things came to a peaceful conclusion in the end, but it was sometimes difficult to know exactly what I should and shouldn't say as I held my own life and, more importantly, the lives of others in the balance.

There was also a really dark and spooky area just off one of the main roads in the Shoreham area that I hated visiting. I think it was a breaker's yard or an old bus station as there were hundreds of broken down vehicles within the compound. We often patrolled through the compound at night and always seemed to see people hanging around, at any time of night. They were obviously up to no good but what they were doing I couldn't tell you. There were people living in some old caravans at the site as well but I don't think they had permission to be there. It was as if the whole place had been deserted and abandoned and the local criminal underworld had taken up residence. The whole place gave me the creeps and I became really jumpy whenever we had to drive in there. My staff realised this and one night some of them hid in the shadows of the yard as I was driven there by a co-conspirator. Just as we were talking about how spooky the place was, my other staff members jumped out of their hiding places, scaring the living daylights out of me. Hilarious!

Acting as a sergeant gave me the opportunity to work on a very basic idea I had to use when searching for vulnerable missing people. The policy at Shoreham at the time was to place as many officers as possible on patrol alone in their vehicles (single patrol) to allow them to attend more incidents and probably to create the impression that there were more police on the ground than there were! In practice this didn't work as members of the public wanted to see police officers actually walking around, not speeding past them in police vehicles. It also caused problems when handling radio equipment and mobile phones as it became illegal to drive when using them.

But I was able to use this crewing policy to my advantage when searching for missing people. On receiving a report of a missing person, my staff were trained to call up on their radios offering to search north, south, east or west from the last known location of the missing person. Obviously the first officer available would go to the person reporting the incident. We had some success with this as it became more organised over time. The natural temptation for officers is for all of them to go to the scene of the incident or to search specific spots where they think the person might be as they want to be the one who finds them and potentially save their life, and so receive the recognition. However, it was necessary for them to resist this temptation and work as a team, travelling to their assigned search areas in order to ensure a thorough search.

One of our most successful cases resulted from a call one evening to report a suspicious man. On arriving and locating the man we discovered some odd items in his possession which related to an address in the Shoreham area and we found some other items that he had thrown on the ground nearby. We found a few vehicles that looked as if they had been interfered with, so arrested him on suspicion of tampering with them. However, as we were transporting the man to custody, an emergency call came in for a burglary at a house. The address seemed familiar and sure enough it matched the address on the property from the prisoner. We had caught and arrested a burglar and recovered the stolen property before the victim had discovered the burglary. You can imagine how impressed they were when we turned up after a few minutes with their property to inform them that we also had a suspect in custody! Unfortunately, this type of thing was a rarity to be savoured.

One of the most dangerous moments of my career also occurred when I was acting at Shoreham. We had been called to attend a domestic dispute, a fairly standard type of call. The man at the address was very tall and heavily built, and I was working with another female officer. Having ascertained that the man had assaulted his female partner at the address, we had no alternative but to arrest him as that was the policy of the force in domestic violence cases. (I understand this has now changed.) The man took exception to the idea that he was about to be arrested and informed us in no uncertain terms that he was not going to allow this to happen. He bolted for the front door which we narrowly managed to prevent by leaning heavily against it whilst trying to restrain him. My colleague then decided to spray the man with Captor in an effort to subdue him, but this didn't really work and all three of us suffered the effects of it as we leaned against the door wheezing and trying to gulp air. To my horror, the man then managed to begin to get the door open and eventually, after fighting with us for a few minutes, succeeded in exiting and running towards the flight of steps outside with both of us hanging on to him for dear life.

You see, it is ingrained into police officers from the moment they join the force that there is no greater crime than allowing an arrested prisoner to escape. I recalled an incident a few years previously when two colleagues lost a robber they were transporting as somehow he managed to jump over the high wall at Brighton police station. Everybody was involved in the search, including the police helicopter and officers from other areas, and nobody was allowed to go home until the prisoner was re-captured. The officers got into a lot of trouble over the incident. In that case it actually worked in our favour as when the prisoner was found, he was at an address with some of the property stolen during the original robbery, but this in no way compensated for the mistake.

Actually, in some circumstances (including this domestic dispute), it was a crazy and very dangerous rule. Fortunately, my colleague had kept her head and shouted, "Let him go," realising that we were both about to be dragged down the flight of stairs. Instinct kicked in as we simultaneously let go and my colleague shouted into her radio for backup. We chased the man down the stairs and into a car park area.

By this point I had recovered myself enough to remember that I also had Captor spray although I had never used it. I drew my Captor and then paused for a few seconds to work out how to use it. I saw the man about to open the door of a car and knew we couldn't allow this. I shouted at him that if he opened the door, I would spray him. He ignored me and I sprayed him several times. Surprisingly, it was a good shot right in the face, as I was pretty worked up from the events leading up to this point. The man immediately began groaning and reaching around, blinded by the spray, as we rushed in, gained control of him and took him to the ground. It was at this point that all of the other officers arrived. I was told that "the world and his wife" were on the way. We watched with satisfaction as six male officers took control of the man who was by now compliant. Afterwards we both felt totally exhausted as the adrenaline wore off and we realised how dangerous the situation had been.

Throughout my career I always tried to avoid media attention or interviews, especially photographs and video footage. I knew that a mistake could follow me around for a long time as I had seen it happen to other officers. I didn't mind my name being in the paper, in fact on occasion I felt quite proud to see it in print, especially when there had been a successful outcome on one of my cases, but I drew the line at photographs. It was at Shoreham when I was acting as sergeant that my quiet and peaceful life out of the public eye came temporarily to an end. My Chief Inspector (the big boss) called me into his office one day to advise that he had set up a photo opportunity for the local newspaper, "The Argus". He wanted to run a story about kids carrying BB Guns and how they could be mistaken for real guns. I began to wonder why he was telling me all of this until he dropped the bombshell, that he wasn't available for the photo opportunity as "something had come up" and he needed me to stand in as the duty sergeant. I protested but in the end had to comply.

So it was that a full page picture of me in uniform holding a range of BB Guns and looking deadly serious ended up on the front page of the local paper, much to the delight of everyone who knew me. The headline was "Armed police seize fake guns from teen gang". I wasn't even armed as I hate guns and would never have applied for the firearms unit, but this didn't seem to matter. As if this wasn't humiliating enough, I arrived at work to find that my team had made numerous copies of the picture and article and stuck them up in every possible location in the police station. Outside work, I was asked if I was one of "Charlie's Angels" for weeks and was told that I looked good in uniform. Looking back it seems quite funny and I've obtained permission from "The Argus" newspaper to use the picture for the front cover of this book, but at the time I was totally embarrassed!

My acting as a sergeant at Shoreham came to an abrupt end when I unexpectedly failed my sergeant's exam. Police exams were not at all based on experience or ability to do the job but entirely on ability to memorise written material and to say specific 'buzz' words in an interview. I had passed the written exams a while back but failed my first attempt at the interview board, despite having been given a good written recommendation by my supervisor. I was frustrated by this and knowing that I wouldn't be allowed to remain in the role long-term now that I didn't have the required qualifications, I requested that I step down and return to CID.

Looking back, this was probably a bad decision; it certainly caused a lot of problems with my supervisor who didn't have anyone to replace me straight away, but at the time I also had an injury to my foot and had been placed on restricted duties but was still required to work night shifts with my team. Being an active sergeant, I liked to go out on patrol and attend as many incidents as possible with my officers but now I was confined to the police station. My supervisor later said that he would have left me in the role longer term even without the approval of the interview board, to allow me to re-apply after twelve months, but at the time I didn't realise this or didn't believe it could happen and thought that the minute someone else came along who was qualified, I would be out. I think I was just so frustrated by my interview failure that I felt I had to do something else.

Later I told a senior colleague that I believed God was in control of the timing of all these things and was shocked when, abandoning all attempts at political correctness, he showed his contempt for my statement by using a four letter word and advising me that this was "rubbish". However, when I calmed down and had a chance to think about things, I knew that what I had said was true, especially in light of events that subsequently transpired.

# CHAPTER THIRTY

# Conflict

Being a supervisor brings conflict that is not generally experienced at a lower level. I had more than my fair share of this, perhaps because I placed my own expectations onto others who probably had different priorities. It is also hard to tread the line between being a supervisor and also a team member. Sometimes I managed teams that had had very lenient supervisors in the past who had become their "buddy" and it was very hard to change this attitude. I wanted to gain the respect and trust of my staff and to be able to socialise with them at times but also I wanted to maintain standards of work, which I couldn't do if I became too friendly with them. I knew that as far as my own experience went I would do anything for a supervisor whom I liked and who had earned my trust and respect. This had to be built up over time; it didn't just come with the title.

I was known as a supervisor who had high standards and implemented them, but also as someone who expected too much at times. Over the years I tried to correct the imbalance but often made mistakes which sometimes damaged relationships. As I became more confident in my role, I learnt to admit my mistakes to my staff and found that most conflicts could be resolved through discussion. Some conflicts occurred because of internal procedures and sometimes I found it difficult to implement the force policy, especially when I didn't agree with it myself. In relation to one of our rules about dealing with missing persons, and using an expression I will always remember, a

127

staff member said to me forcefully one day, "But Sergeant, that's just bureaucratic nonsense," and I had to agree with him. In fact, some of the things we did on a daily basis were just that.

In the earlier chapter "Wasting Police Time" I mentioned that there was a specific way that reports should be written in order to ensure they were accepted for filing (no further investigation needed). Some officers quickly cottoned on to this idea and learnt the method required, but others didn't. The outcome was that these officers wrote their reports, usually using long and detailed descriptions which they thought would hide their omissions, without actually saying whether a crime had or hadn't occurred, or stating that a crime hadn't occurred when it was obvious from reading the content of the report that it had. Often I found these reports extremely amusing as, when reading them, it was immediately obvious to me what had actually happened and, knowing the filing system, the reason why the officer had written a different version of events.

One officer wrote a huge essay about an assault allegation he had attended, but when I looked closely at what he had written, it was obvious that he hadn't actually spoken to the alleged victim, probably because he knew she would make an assault allegation. This avoidance of recording crime may sound strange to a non-police reader, but it was understandable as we often dealt with serial complainers who later withdrew their statements or turned against us when they became "friends" with the suspect again, leaving our case at a standstill – until the following week, that is, when they had had another drunken falling out. So in non-domestic violence cases it was sometimes six of one and half a dozen of the other and a total waste of police time.

Usually the best way to deal with these report failings was to ask specific questions of the officer and if they were evasive, to tell them that it wasn't a believable version of events and that if I didn't believe it, the people filing the reports wouldn't either. Then I asked them either to re-write the report or to get more information or, as a last resort, to re-attend and deal with the incident as per the guidelines. I felt sorry for officers like this at times as they were just trying to emulate their colleagues but didn't have the skill to do so. Sometimes we were just following a process rather than solving crime as the cases weren't going anywhere, so I understood their frustration when they had been asked to re-write their report for the fifth time. I couldn't allow these reports to be sent for filing as I knew they would be rejected by the Crime Recording Information Assistants (CRIAs). This role was created during the "Wasting Police Time" era and the force seemed to employ the most bureaucratic individuals to fulfil this responsibility.

"Victim contracts" were another bureaucratic measure brought in to try to ensure officers updated victims about the progress of their reports of crime at specific times in the investigation. In principle the idea was a good one, but in practice the way they operated when they were first implemented didn't work. When a victim reported a crime, the attending officer was to ask them how often and at which stage of the investigation they wanted to be updated and then to record this on the crime report. Basic details of all crime reports were on our computer system and a traffic light system was used to show whether a victim had been updated on time or not. The problem was that some victims were unrealistic with their expectations; they asked to be updated twice a week by phone. This was impossible straightaway as the officer wouldn't be on duty to comply with the request and some of their shifts would be night shifts. For some reason, fulfilment of these contracts became the highest measure of performance for senior officers and they spent huge amounts of time chasing them up and berating officers who failed to comply.

I was reviewing officers' reports in my office when one officer placed an extra report in my tray for filing. I asked him whether he had updated the victim with the outcome and he stated that he had. When I checked the report, I saw that he had written that he had updated the victim during his shift that day, but he had a night shift starting at 11pm. I approached him and asked, "How did you update this victim today when we are on nights?" Fortunately for him, one of my other staff overheard our discussion, saw that he was about to make a colossal mistake, and jumped in with, "Be careful what you say because you are trapped!"

Sergeants were also required to carry out Victim Satisfaction surveys which involved phoning a victim our officers had dealt with and asking them questions about the "service provided". This was another measure which wasted hours of supervisory time as we frantically phoned round hundreds of people only to find that they couldn't remember having contacted the police in the first place, or didn't want to talk to us, or demanded to know where we had got their numbers from. When we did manage to carry out the surveys, we usually skipped over an embarrassingly awkward question to find out if they were "completely", "very", or "fairly" satisfied. Most people we contacted were unable to make this distinction.

The most amusing disciplinary type incident I can recall was when I asked to speak with one of my staff as I was leaving the office one day. He responded that it wasn't possible for me to speak with him as I had already removed my tie, meaning (in his mind) that I was no longer on duty and therefore not entitled to speak with him!

# CHAPTER THIRTY-ONE

# Gay Pride Parade

It was also at Shoreham that, unfortunately, I found myself on the other side of a disciplinary investigation. As I write this chapter I know that it will be the most controversial. I have excluded a lot of detail in the interest of everyone involved. It is not my intention to expose anyone or to express resentment about anything that occurred. I believe mistakes were made and it is my hope that if a similar situation were to occur in the future, there might be a different outcome.

After I turned back to my Christian faith in 2005, I became involved in my local church and developed a passion for reaching out to others. In the Bible, Jesus gives all Christians a clear instruction to "...go and make disciples of all nations" (Matthew 28:19, NIV). I began to share my faith with colleagues at work whenever opportunities arose. However, after a while I was called into my inspector's office to be reminded that "maybe people don't want to hear about your faith all of the time". I asked whether he had ever said that to a male officer about football, which ended the discussion fairly promptly!

I regularly took part in street evangelism in my local town of Worthing. On Saturday mornings a small team from my church met for prayer and then went to allocated spots in the town to give out leaflets about Christianity and to talk to people, sharing our faith. We received mixed reactions ranging from people asking for prayer and details of the church, to people threatening violence as they tore up the leaflets and stomped on them. We were reminded by our pastor that people were not angry with or rejecting us, but God, which helped to make it less personal.

One Saturday I was asked if I wanted to go to the neighbouring town of Brighton to join some members from my church and other churches in the area to conduct a peaceful protest at the annual Gay Pride Parade event. I was aware of the event due to the large police operation requiring months of planning in advance every year for safety and security. I had never been involved in policing the event but I had been informed by other officers that it was a particularly tough duty due to the long hours and the behaviour of some of the attendees. Representatives and participants of the local gay community took part in a parade through the city centre to celebrate "being gay".

As a Christian I knew that the Bible teaches us to love people regardless of their lifestyle choices and behaviour. After the life I had lived, I couldn't judge others, especially those that weren't making claims to be Christian. I had supervised gay officers and one of my closest female colleagues was gay. I tried to treat people as individuals and to get to know them, rather than thinking of them in terms of their sexuality. However, an organised event such as Gay Pride specifically to celebrate this lifestyle was something different. I couldn't in good conscience endorse it. Some officers disliked policing the event due to the drunkenness, nakedness, lewdness, crudeness and general debauchery that often took place. They also resented being told to make exceptions and relax the law for the revellers. Some officers with families also felt that this simply wasn't an environment for children and yet others chose to make the event a family day out. Just a few years before, gay police officers had been given permission to join the main parade and to march in uniform in duty time. They were encouraged to do this by those in senior positions within the force.

The parade was due to take place on one of my days off so I agreed to participate in the peaceful protest, not really knowing what would be involved. I had previously attended pro-life events standing for hours at the side of the road holding banners with Bible verses on them so I guessed this would be similar. I was told that the local police had been informed and had given permission for the demonstration. We would stand in a police designated area and hold banners with Bible verses on them. I agreed with the principle behind the protest and knew it would be peaceful so I didn't foresee a problem. It didn't really cross my mind that there would be a conflict with my role as a police officer as I was off duty and there was nothing to identify me as an officer. As far as the people were concerned I was just a member of a local Christian church attending the event in my spare time.

On arrival at the parade area, with about twelve others, I realised that this was a really huge event as I saw thousands of people milling around and we were being pushed along with the crowd. We were ushered onto a patch of grass and there were a lot of people heading in our direction. A few police officers were scattered around and I saw several whom I knew. I gave out Gospel leaflets; as far as I was concerned, getting the Gospel to the people at the event was the priority, over and above the protest.

Later, I was asked to hold a banner which had the message of salvation from John 3:16 (NIV):

> "For God so loved the world that he gave his one and only
> Son, that whoever believes in him shall not perish but have
> eternal life."

An eighty-five-year-old navy veteran was at the event with us, giving out leaflets containing his testimony. He inspired all of us. He was reaching out to the gay people who respected him due to his service and several had photos taken with him. They saw him as a frail and confused old man, but I knew that his mind was still sharp and that he was desperately praying for these people and trying to reach them for the Gospel. He was really very brave to attend this event, especially with the specific intention to share the Gospel, as he could easily have been trampled in the crowd or attacked by those who resented his message.

As we held our banners, one of the men in our group began preaching with a loudspeaker. We began to feel the hostility of the crowd who were standing waiting for the parade. It started with them asking and then shouting questions at us which we tried to answer respectfully, but gradually it turned to abuse and arguing. After the parade floats had gone past, the crowd that was following them became angry. They were cursing and shouting and started throwing things in our direction. I sensed that the situation was getting out of control and, even with my police training, I felt afraid being on the other side for a change.

The police, who had been very respectful and polite throughout, formed a loose cordon around us (they stood in a line holding onto each other's belts with their backs to us to protect us from the crowd). But the crowd threw glass beer bottles at us and several people were struck, including an old man in our group. The police struggled to hold onto the cordon as people tried to break through and get to us. The whole situation was very scary. In the end, after about ten minutes, the police advised us that it was time for us to leave as we had been there several hours already and they were afraid that they wouldn't be able to protect us from the thousands of angry people who were becoming more aggressive as they consumed more alcohol. Most of us agreed with this and were grateful to the police for what they had done, although a few of our number complained that they had the right to protest and wanted to stay. I knew that the police were genuinely concerned for our safety and I had no issues with being asked to leave early. In fact, I was shocked at the turn of events and the hostility of the crowd. We were escorted away by the police to the sound of the jeers from the crowd.

Later I reflected on what had happened, wondering whether it had been worth it as we had had little time to actually give out tracts and share the Gospel; I wondered if anyone was listening to us when we had. I thought that was the end of the matter and put it behind me.

On arriving for work a few days later, I realised that things were not normal due to the way people were behaving towards me. I received a phone call from a senior officer requesting a meeting to discuss my presence at the event. I was asked questions about my presence and intentions and about a specific religious group to which I had no connection. The officer asked me how I felt now that ten thousand people in Brighton "hated" me. I was surprised as I didn't see any reason for people to even know my identity. The senior officer stated that there would be consequences to my behaviour. I asked what these might be but was told there would be discussions at a higher level and decisions would be made and communicated to me in due course. I was left believing that my job was on the line and that there was nothing I could do about it. I was devastated as I enjoyed my job and saw my career with Sussex Police as my long-term future, but I knew that if called upon to do so, I would have to put my faith first and trust that God would protect me.

I contacted my Police Federation (police union) who, on hearing of the circumstances, supported my right to attend the event. They pointed out that if officers were allowed to march in uniform in duty time as part of the event, then I must be allowed to take part in a peaceful protest in my own time, otherwise there was no equality. They told me that there was case law supporting the view. I was relieved and surprised that a secular organisation had come to my aid and would defend my stance, albeit on the grounds of equality not Biblical truth. The Federation also asked some gay officers for their views and, perhaps surprisingly, they supported my right to be present at the event.

After numerous meetings and discussions I was told that some people considered my views "abhorrent" and that I had "made an error in judgement in aligning [myself] with a minority group in public". The suggestion was that although I had not in fact discriminated against anyone, I had the potential to in the future because of my views. Personally I felt that I was being asked to choose between my faith and my career with Sussex Police. I began making plans to resign rather than compromise my faith.

In the middle of this fiasco, while many of my colleagues continued to treat me as an alien in their midst, I was called to another meeting. I assumed it would be a continuation of the previous matter, as I considered it still unresolved, but instead I was informed that a decision had been made to move me from Shoreham to a new station. I was surprised to hear this but even more surprised when they informed me that they were transferring me to Brighton, the very place where allegedly I had ten thousand enemies! It was to be a forcible transfer effective immediately. The reason given was that I had been selected "at random" from the CID department as they were trying to fill vacancies in northern areas of the force by moving Brighton officers into them. They then needed to backfill the Brighton slots. Off the record, doubts were expressed about the reasons given.

At the end of my tether, I made one final request to try to save my career as I was not prepared to move to Brighton in the circumstances. I requested a meeting with someone very senior. To my surprise this was agreed, and the meeting was conducive. I was able to explain my views and reassure the force on several counts. Although the senior officer didn't agree with me, he accepted that I was entitled to hold my Christian views as everyone has personal views about a whole range of subjects. He accepted that I couldn't be held accountable for something that I might or might not do in the future. He agreed that it was exceptionally bad timing for me to be transferred to Brighton and he understood my concerns about this.

In return I offered a compromise; I was willing to be directly transferred to one of the stations in the north of the force which would fill the vacancies they were attempting to fill in the first place. This was a good compromise all round as it would give me a new start at a new station away from all the gossip and rumours and would help the force with their staffing issues to the north. I was assuming when I made the offer that I would be transferred to Horsham which was a twenty-five minute drive from home but in the end I was sent to Crawley, forty-five minutes away.

On reflection of the whole situation, which was the most difficult period of my service, one of the reasons for the hostility amongst fellow officers was a misrepresentation of my views at all levels and no attempt was made to correct the misrepresentations at a senior level. Some (not all) senior officers inadvertently encouraged the hostility by treating me as if I were "homophobic" or had done something worthy of discipline, which made things a lot worse as officers tried to distance themselves from me in case they were caught up in the fall-out that they believed would one day come. I believe now that a lot of it was to do with fear as the force struggled to handle new territory and a situation with which they were uncomfortable and unfamiliar.

I was given assurances later that the stand I had taken was worthwhile from a Christian perspective as procedures were changed to ensure the force would in future deal differently with a similar situation. Although I was glad to hear this, it didn't mend the broken friendships or heal the pain of being misunderstood in so many ways over this issue.

# CHAPTER THIRTY-TWO

# A New Start

I enjoyed my time at Crawley working in a small team with a sergeant of a similar age to me with whom I got on well. She commented that it must feel like I was throwing "tenners" out of the window of my car every time I drove to work. It did feel a bit like that at first but I grudgingly accepted it as I knew I needed to knuckle down and make an impression at Crawley CID; I still had hopes for permanent promotion once the prior incident had died down, now that my job was no longer under threat! The rumours from south of the force either hadn't reached the ears of those in the north or they had decided to give me the benefit of the doubt. Either way, I was grateful that I didn't have to face any of the hostility previously encountered.

It was at Crawley that some officers had lists of random words that they tried to insert into taped police interviews, sometimes even with defence solicitors present. Police interviews can often be a formality as there is usually a discussion between the solicitor and police officer before the interview and most of the time an indication is given at this stage as to what will be said. Therefore they can become tedious, especially as it is necessary to work through a set legal procedure regardless of the anticipated outcome.

The word game definitely made the interviews more interesting and was never used in cases that were resting on an interview or where the interview was important. It was cases where the interview was a legal formality and everyone knew it. I wasn't very good at the game. One day my male colleague said the word "googleberrys" before trying unsuccessfully to cover it with a cough as the solicitor said, "I'm sorry, what?" and the defendant looked confused. I developed a fit of hysterics and couldn't control it. I was forced to pretend that I was laughing about something completely unrelated to the interview and vowed never to put myself in that position again.

Crawley was a whole different ballgame to my previous stations; I was informed of whole streets being "danger" areas that shouldn't be entered alone. I think this was due to its proximity to London and the travelling criminals who sometimes crossed local borders. One of the first cases I worked on was an arson with intent to endanger life, the suspect having placed a burning piece of material through a letterbox with the occupants sleeping inside the property. Shortly after this I was dealing with a case involving one of the "most dangerous criminals" in Sussex who was somehow managing to co-ordinate serious criminal activity using mobile telephones he had smuggled into his prison cell. Every time a "cell raid" was conducted to locate the phones, they were mysteriously nowhere to be found.

Another time we stopped a driver who claimed to be a student on his way back from university, but on searching his vehicle we discovered a large bag of cannabis in the boot. In the interior there was a professional kit for breaking into vehicles, a stun gun and some other less interesting items. In the door pocket there was a metal pen that looked like a fountain pen or similar but the weight of it suggested otherwise. On closer examination by our specialists, we were informed that it was actually a "pen gun" capable of firing a lethal bullet and that it was the first discovery of such an item within our police force. Possession of such an item carried a mandatory five year prison sentence!

Shortly after I arrived at Crawley, I was tasked with the annual review of a report concerning a long-term missing person who was also wanted for an offence. As mentioned in earlier chapters, missing people, especially those missing for a long time, was a subject in which I was very interested. A lot of officers would probably have received this type of case, given a bored sigh and then done the bare minimum to get the case re-filed by a supervisor. In contrast, when I received it, I actually believed it was possible to find the person, and set about trying to do so using all methods at my disposal.

After some initial phone calls and research, I believed the man was possibly living at a previous address, maybe under an assumed name, as someone had started claiming benefits there a few months after the man disappeared. I attended the area of the address with a colleague and spoke to some neighbours. They said they hadn't seen the man for at least a year and that there was never a rubbish collection or anything of that nature. I wanted to enter the actual premises but at this stage there were no grounds to do so as there was no evidence anyone was in there and there was no answer at the door. The flat was on the second floor and there was no way to see inside. I was determined to get in just to make sure, but my colleague thought that it was a dead-end and was concerned about the cost of forcing an entry into the premises. We left to do some other enquiries and then returned to the address later. I was starting to believe it was a lost cause, when I noticed that a very small upstairs bathroom window was open; I was sure it had been closed when we were there just a few hours earlier. As far as I was concerned, that was sufficient to force an entry and so I called for an officer trained in using the door enforcer. My colleague remarked that I would have to explain the cost to our boss later.

We forced the door and immediately saw that the whole place was in complete darkness with windows and light areas blacked out. I didn't know how anyone could live in this environment but I also saw many stacks of tinned food in a corridor and heard a scuffling upstairs. We found the man there, where he had been hiding out for many months, only venturing out occasionally at night to replenish supplies. I told him that people had been looking for him for two years and that they were very worried. He had broken off all contact with his family when he went into hiding and even now wasn't interested in communicating with them, although he gave me permission to tell them that he was alive. He looked deathly pale and quite ill, maybe partly from a lack of daylight and vitamin D. I arrested him and took him to the police station, then relished the surprised look on my inspector's face as I completed the paperwork and gave him back the solved crime file. Another moment to savour, as they were few and far between.

After a while at Crawley, I started to get itchy feet and the daily travelling distance was becoming a problem both financially and in terms of the wasted time. Our team morale was also quite low as we had been informed that one of us was to be forcibly transferred to fill a vacancy in another department that no one wanted to work in. This resulted in most of the officers being considered for the transfer saying that if they were moved, they would apply to leave Sussex Police and transfer to the MET Police in London. This may seem like an empty threat but there was at least one officer in my team who already lived in London and was travelling to Sussex every day and receiving a much lower salary than he would get in the MET. Sussex were in a no-win situation; they had to move someone, but as they selected officers one by one, they either came up with legitimate excuses or transferred out of the force making good their threats. I was glad to be exempted from this procedure as I had by now passed the necessary written exams and learnt the interview technique required to pass the sergeant's exam board so was eligible for promotion.

I applied for a Detective Sergeant's post at Horsham CID as there was an advertised vacancy. However, I was informed some time later that the position had been filled by a more experienced officer within CID. I hadn't been interviewed or even contacted about this after having applied for the position. I did receive an apology later down the line but I was disillusioned by the failure to keep me informed and so turned my attention in a different direction.

# CHAPTER THIRTY-THREE

# Steam Engine

In late 2008, I applied for a Uniformed Sergeant post on Horsham response. I was accepted and was due to take up my new post in early 2009. Prior to beginning, I had my third serious off-duty car accident from which I was fortunate to escape relatively unscathed; my car was not so fortunate and joined my collection of vehicles in the local breaker's yard.

I was travelling back from a weekend away in the Midlands. I was driving in the "fast lane" (lane two) at about seventy miles per hour and had entered a particularly dark stretch of road with no street lighting. The roads were pretty quiet and I couldn't see other vehicles around. Then I saw some orange lights about five hundred metres ahead of me on the side of the road. I assumed the lights belonged to a vehicle that was waiting in a loading bay at the side of the road although I couldn't see a vehicle. Lorry drivers often pulled over on the dual carriageway for their mandatory breaks after driving for many hours. The lights were at least a lane away from me and were stationary so I didn't slow down for them as there was no need.

But as these things subconsciously passed through my mind, suddenly I saw a huge solid wall of grey only about one hundred metres in front of me. It was all I could see and it was completely blocking both lanes. I realised with horror that it was a slow vehicle sideways on to me and crossing the road from the central reservation. There was no time to brake and nowhere to go. I recall thinking, "This is it, I'm going to die, am I ready?" and then I braced myself and hit the rear of the slow-moving vehicle at full-speed. My car spun around and once again glass came crashing in around me, but a few moments later I was able to climb out of the mess of my vehicle virtually unharmed. The road was pitch black and deathly quiet as if it were in shock. I certainly was, although I didn't realise it at the time. The silence was broken by a man rushing towards me, throwing his arms around me and emotionally saying he was sorry and was so glad I was okay. I realised he must have been driving the large slow vehicle which I later learnt was a steam engine returning late from a show.

I busied myself attempting to locate my handbag and other personal items from the remains of my vehicle as people urged me to "forget about" the items and tried to lead me out of the road and away from the crash site. I ended up in the house of the driver of the steam engine drinking a cup of tea with his wife as I attempted in vain to reach my parents on the phone. Ironically, it was Sunday evening and they were at church with their phones switched off. This was a cruel twist as my brother had died on a Sunday evening after he had attended church. I answered the door of the house on hearing the doorbell and two ambulance personnel asked me if they could attend to the person who had been driving the vehicle in the road outside. I informed them that I was the driver but they didn't believe me, as they were expecting serious injuries, until it was confirmed by the others at the house. They told me I was going to hospital and when I protested stating that I was fine, they made it clear that having seen the wreckage of my vehicle, it wasn't an option. I finally got hold of my parents and they agreed to join me at Worthing hospital.

Unbelievably, I suffered little physical ill effect from my near-death experience. I had seatbelt bruising and pain in my chest from the impact for a few weeks. Mentally, however, I was a mess. For at least a week I was in a daze; all of the things that had seemed so important before suddenly seemed irrelevant as I realised the brevity and fragility of life and re-evaluated and took stock of my priorities. I did have flashbacks after the incident and became a nervous driver for a while. I was especially nervous whenever I saw orange lights, especially at night, expecting to see large vehicles emerging from nowhere and blocking my path.

Later I found out that the steam engine driver was a local man and was also a Christian. I had already decided not to sue the insurance company for my injuries as I'm not a big fan of the compensation culture and wanted to put my money where my mouth was. This was despite being bombarded with phone calls from "no win, no fee" lawyers desperate to persuade me otherwise. I wasn't especially interested in seeing the driver prosecuted but I did want to make sure steps were taken to ensure the same thing didn't happen again to someone else. For this reason I supported a prosecution hoping for recommendations to be made regarding lighting on the vehicle, etc. However, after a while the police informed me that it wasn't possible to prosecute the driver as the Steam Engine fell outside Road Traffic Legislation, a fact I still find difficult to believe. I'm sure something would have been done if someone had died. In any event, I was reassured to hear that lighting had been added to the vehicle and I think the driver had suffered enough with the guilt over what had happened.

Someone told me that there had been an accident on the same road in the past in exactly the same circumstances as a long vehicle had blocked the path of two cars travelling on the dual carriageway. In that case, both cars had hit the long vehicle at full speed and all of the occupants had died.

# CHAPTER THIRTY-FOUR

# Traffic Incidents

Several of the most difficult traffic incidents I had to deal with occurred whilst I was stationed at Horsham, probably due to the large network of busy roads in the area. It was probably only then that I noticed that the name of such an incident had been quietly changed from "accident" to "collision", apparently because the politically correct brigade had decided that someone was always at fault in any road "incident", therefore it wasn't an "accident". (My colleague reading the first draft of this book pointed out that it was "accident" to "collision" and not "accident" to "crash" as I had originally written, with the comment that, "Traffic never was your strong point!")

Whatever the reason, it came as no surprise to me as names of departments, procedures and anything else with an official name were frequently changed within the Police Service. This occurred either because the government had decided that we were no longer to dedicate time and resources to a particular matter, in which case the easiest solution was to change the name to allow things to continue as they were, or because someone with far too much time on their hands had complained or suggested a different name for something, which had then been discussed at length over numerous management meetings resulting in a decision to change the status quo. Very rarely was an actual procedure or department changed, just the name, which seemed to satisfy those further up the chain and left those of us lower down in a constant state of confusion as we struggled to keep up.

The knowledge I was acquiring of road traffic law, as I was back working in uniform, did come in handy when I was supervising a crash scene near Henfield. I had asked the first driver in a line of traffic to wait as we cleared the vehicles involved in the accident from the road directly in front of him. He wasn't very happy about this and made this clear to me, but I stuck to my guns and repeated my instruction. He complied for a few minutes but then when I turned my back to the queue of traffic, he put his foot down suddenly and shot forward, making his way around the accident scene and off up the road, followed by several other vehicles that had been behind him in the queue. I wrote down his registration number and determined not to let the matter go as I stopped the traffic again as per my original plan.

On returning to the station, I sent a summons to the driver's home address for failing to comply with an instruction given by a police officer in uniform. I had never heard of this law but the traffic department had been suitably impressed by my desire to do something about the infringement and had therefore assisted me. After a few days, I received a letter from the man giving a medical reason for the infringement and asking me to consider dropping the case against him. I decided to be lenient in the circumstances but wrote him a long letter advising him of the consequences of his actions and the dangers of being so reckless.

I was grateful that I had not had to deal with a lot of serious road or rail incidents as I heard details from my opposite number, based at Pulborough, of people jumping in front of trains and a falling tree branch killing a passing driver outright. I did, however, have to deliver a message to the family of a young male driver who was in critical condition at a local hospital, having been involved in a crash. Knowing on a personal level how they must be feeling, passing on the message was really tough and made worse when the traffic department advised that they had no officers free to drive the family to the hospital. In the end, the victim's very young sister offered to drive the family and we had to allow this as there was no viable alternative.

Since the death of my brother in 2002, I had avoided dealing with serious road crashes where possible and was lacking in experience in this type of accident. Actually, this was often a problem for sergeants who switched from CID to uniform as we knew exactly how to manage a major crime scene for a murder or rape but struggled with basic tasks like issuing traffic tickets and public order warnings. I would rather it was this way round, though, as sergeants who went from uniform to CID at first felt as if they were floundering when they were plunged into the deep end, taking charge of serious incidents before they were really ready.

The first serious traffic crash occurred soon after I had arrived at Horsham when I began supervising my new team. One of my officers crashed a police vehicle in the middle of the town centre at a road junction near to some shops. The driver was injured and trapped in the vehicle. He was obviously in severe pain from an injury he had sustained to his leg. His crew-mate was also injured and needed medical attention. The driver's off-duty partner (also a police officer and on my team) then arrived at the scene and became understandably emotional. My team consisted of only five officers.

Members of the public had gathered and were refusing to leave the area despite being asked to do so. They insisted on standing as close as possible to the police tape cordon that had been set up and were insensitively taking photos and videos of the incident. I resisted the urge to shout at them to leave as I knew they had the right to be there. I could feel my blood pressure rising as their presence was the last thing I needed. I wanted to protect my colleagues who were visibly in pain and probably didn't want the photos of their anguish plastered onto numerous social media networks later in the day.

The accident occurred in the worst possible place: at a junction in a busy town centre. It was every new sergeant's nightmare scenario, even more so for someone who had spent almost their entire service within CID as a detective, and I had no idea what to do at the scene of a major collision, let alone a police accident. Fortunately, one of the two remaining officers had some idea of what to do and started placing road signs around the scene. At any incident like this it was always a relief when the Traffic Department (later changed to Road Policing Department) arrived and agreed to take control of things.

I was rushing around barking orders but didn't have much clue as to what I was doing. In hindsight I realise I was also upset by the injuries, both physical and emotional, to three of my team. My responsibility was firstly to them and this left me with little capacity to think rationally about preserving the accident scene. The contrast between myself and the calm, collected traffic officers as they discussed the scene was stark. I think they saw the burden I was carrying as they were exceptionally helpful and agreed to provide their own officers to take over from us completely. This wasn't normal practice so I was grateful to them in the circumstances.

They immediately widened the cordon and closed off the entire road network, which gave us the time and space to breathe and to investigate properly, something we should have done in the first place. I had been too concerned about getting the traffic flowing again and not wanting to inconvenience people. After forty-five minutes an ambulance finally arrived and the officers went to hospital. All later made a full recovery but I was left reeling as I realised how little I knew about traffic incidents and how difficult it had been to stay emotionally detached when dealing with my own staff in a traumatic situation.

Traffic situations were not always a negative experience and were sometimes highly entertaining. One of the most ridiculous calls we received was during the heavy snowfall in the winter of 2009. This was a time when many officers didn't make it into work or were very late as they were snowed in and those who did arrive enjoyed being ferried around en masse in the small number of 4x4 vehicles that Sussex Police owned. We received a report of a "stuck ambulance", so another sergeant and I jumped in a 4x4 and rushed (or slid) out of the station to go and assist our close colleagues. I'm not sure if it is the same across the country, but locally we tended to have a very close working relationship with ambulance personnel, more so than with the fire brigade whom we overlapped with less regularly.

On arrival I saw that the ambulance had become stuck in a residential area on an icy road with a slight build-up of snow in front of it. On getting out and surveying the scene for a few seconds, I noted that the area behind the ambulance and the path it had taken to get into its current predicament was essentially clear. I hesitated and checked around for something I must have missed before I risked making a complete fool of myself and asked the obvious question: "Have you tried reversing?" The answer when it came astonished both me and my colleague and also seemed to be a light bulb moment for the now very embarrassed ambulance crew as they hastened back to the comfort and warmth of their vehicle to follow the advice of their also now very-embarrassed-on-their-behalf police colleagues.

We watched expressionless, as anything else may have been misconstrued, as they quickly reversed away from the small snow drift and turned their vehicle around ready for their next assignment. Prior to resuming their duties, in a gesture which I totally appreciated, the male member of the crew, now humiliated, hid his face behind his hands as they both thanked us for our "assistance" and bumbled away. I hastily contacted our control room via my radio to cancel the additional resources we had on standby, including a recovery vehicle, and gave a verbal update as follows: "Police attended, ambulance was stuck, advice given to reverse, ambulance reversed, problem solved, we are standing down!"

# CHAPTER THIRTY-FIVE

# Driving Course, Again

An embarrassing personal failure had occurred when I attended my three week driving course in 2002 in an attempt to obtain a licence to drive with blue lights and two tones (sirens). Most officers who failed this course failed the written theory exam during the first week. I passed the theory with flying colours but I failed the practical driving course. I was told afterwards that my instructor didn't like young women or probationary officers. However, I did find the course very difficult and was nervous throughout. On returning to division, a colleague remarked that he had never heard of anyone failing the practical exam, which made me feel a lot better! I didn't retake this course until much later in 2009 partly due to working in plain clothed specialist roles where it wasn't necessary but also due to the death of my brother and the avoidance of all things "traffic" for a period of time.

Whilst stationed at Horsham I was given the opportunity to repeat my driving course at HQ, Lewes. The course was now a month long instead of just three weeks and most of the former instructors had moved on. For the first three weeks we were driving plain vehicles around the entire force area to experience different driving conditions and the final week was the pursuit training in the marked police vehicles. I was still nervous due to my previous experience but was determined to succeed on my second attempt. I enjoyed the course this time, although it was demanding as we were pushed to reach extremely

149

high speeds at times and I had to develop a totally new driving technique.

I also took the van course and so found myself uncomfortably driving what seemed to me to be a huge windowless vehicle along some of the county's roads praying that I wouldn't lose control of it. The instructors had deliberately blacked out the windows so that we had to learn to use our mirrors properly. After this, driving a 4x4, also part of the final week of the course, was easy.

On one day we went to the skid pan which the guys in my team absolutely loved but which I decided not to participate in after developing severe sickness after just a few runs. The skid pan, which reminded me of something from Top Gear, is basically a large area, rather like a large empty car park or a huge playground, on which to practise driving at high speeds and then suddenly stopping and attempting to deal properly with the resulting skid. It wasn't a compulsory part of the course and although I would have liked to participate, my body said otherwise and I found that I couldn't continue. I passed another exercise, a kind of assault course involving driving around cones. The best approach for this was to be slow and steady but as we were also up against the clock, it was extremely challenging and there were many crashes, although we all did enough to pass.

The pursuit training in the marked vehicles was something else. Learning to communicate via the in-car radio whilst coordinating lights and sirens and actually driving the vehicle was tough. Other drivers could also be an inconvenience as they often did things that were unexpected. One driver in the first lane of the dual carriageway suddenly signalled and pulled out right in front of me as I was attempting to pass her at a speed of over 100mph. I also felt embarrassed by the attention the sirens drew to the vehicle, especially in built up areas. It felt like every eye was watching my driving and expecting it to be perfect because I was in a police vehicle. The most difficult thing was having to make sure we were out of sight of any members of the public before switching the lights and sirens off as they may have been a bit annoyed to realise it was just a training exercise and that we were not in fact attending an emergency.

The pursuit scenarios were the most dramatic and amusing as our instructors dressed up as "criminals" driving normal vehicles and our task was to pursue and catch them using the marked cars whilst accompanied by another instructor. We had a near miss straight away. One of my male colleagues was driving and he got caught up in the moment when he was pursuing his "suspect" along a main road in the overtaking lane as he approached a roundabout. The suspect, who was in the first lane, suddenly and without indication took the first exit on the roundabout and shot off up a side road to the left. The police trainee driver, still in the overtaking lane but with tunnel vision, shot after him, narrowly avoiding crashing into the other vehicles which were patiently waiting (as all British drivers do) in the first lane for an opportunity to navigate the roundabout.

We were given the pursuit scenarios on paper before the pursuits started so we had some idea of what we might be dealing with. When it was my turn, my paper said that I was chasing a teenager who had stolen his dad's car and was taking it on a joyride. I followed the "suspect" vehicle for a long time thinking that maybe my opportunity had passed as I hadn't been able to catch up with him as he was driving too fast but then he got stuck in traffic. I was about ten cars behind him but could still see him, so in the end I jumped out and rushed to the driver's side of his car. I then grabbed the keys from the ignition as, fortunately, his window was open. I was preparing to drag him out of the vehicle when it became apparent he had come out of role, having decided that it was time to end the role play which was creating a bit of a stir as it was broad daylight in the middle of heavy traffic in a busy area. Many eyes were now focused on us, especially as we were both now laughing. In my mind I imagined the necessary press release to explain the incident to the public at a later stage. Apparently my actions were sufficient, although it wasn't what the instructors had anticipated when they planned the scenarios!

Some of the more hair-raising moments during the main course in the plain cars occurred as other students made heart-stopping mistakes which could very easily have gotten us all killed. One trainee pulled out of a quiet junction onto a busy main road narrowly missing two cars travelling in opposite directions at around seventy miles per hour. As our instructor shakily advised her to pull over at the next lay-by, incredibly, she informed us that she hadn't seen either of the other vehicles. Another student, during her final check drive, shot across a crossroads without stopping, having failed to realise the junction was there.

The biggest mistake I made which, fortunately, wasn't counted against me was on the very last day of the course, the day on which the instructors would be making the final decisions about whether to pass or fail us. The instructors took great pride in the training cars we were driving around in and so every day both before and after use, to teach us good disciplinary practice, we were forced to wash the vehicles properly, inspect them for damage, check the fluid levels and generally to look after them. A teammate and I were tasked with collecting our vehicle from the underground car park, something that we did every day. Confidently, I got into the driver's seat and my teammate sat in the back of the vehicle as we continued chatting to each other. Then I turned the key in the ignition as the vehicle shot backwards and with a loud bang crashed into the wall behind us as the engine stalled. I had forgotten the golden rule which had been drummed into us every day for the entire course: make sure the vehicle has not been left in gear. I sat in stunned silence thinking I had blown all my chances as my teammate started to roar with laughter. Other officers, including an instructor who "just happened" to be in the car park at the time, came running over as I sheepishly got out of the vehicle to inspect the damage, which I assumed would be bad.

The others were already checking the impact point as I joined them looking for the inevitable dent or scrape that would surely bring an end to my hopes of passing for the second time. Surprisingly there was only a very tiny dent that could barely be seen, which was in no way proportionate to the loud bang that had brought everyone running. I looked at the instructor willing him not to pass on what he knew of the unfortunate incident to my own instructor who wasn't there. Instead, and to my relief, he jokingly made a comment similar to, "I like chocolate!" In the end my instructor did find out but that didn't seem to influence his decision and so finally I passed my driving course on the second attempt, more than five years after the first failed attempt. I couldn't wait to get back to Horsham to practise my newly acquired skill. Drivers, beware!

# CHAPTER THIRTY-SIX

# Settling Down – Horsham

After passing my driving course, I settled back into life at Horsham. I was still getting to know my team and sometimes having to deal with the resulting conflict, but in general I enjoyed the role. I especially enjoyed teasing some of my staff about their spelling and grammatical errors or about the way they had incorrectly worded reports for one reason or another. I would sometimes read the errors out loud from my office so that other officers could hear, to encourage them to laugh at their own silly mistakes, and often they did. One serial offender even started coming to me to show me his mistakes before he had submitted his reports just so I could laugh at them!

Another officer being supervised by a sergeant colleague continued investigating a non-criminal matter of nuisance phone calls, long after he had been told to finalise it. He was desperate to seek justice for his victim, even though both of us, as sergeants, told him he was wasting his time as the case wasn't going anywhere. This was a rare occurrence as mostly officers were desperate to get rid of dead-end cases, not hanging on to them for dear life. We didn't want to kill his enthusiasm and had to admire his diligence but there came a point when enough was enough and he needed to focus on something else. However, this was the same officer who sent a request to our technical department for a CCTV tape to be copied, and somehow ended up receiving back three thick books of CCTV still photos instead, likely due to serious

153

errors made on the request form. He also accidentally sent an email to the entire force about the door at his very small country station of Pulborough being stuck. Some of the replies cannot be repeated but the more amusing ones included, "Why are you telling me this?" "Where is Pulborough?" "I don't care!" and, "Shouldn't you be rounding up sheep?"

I practised my emergency driving carefully at first, but found that I really grew to enjoy it. I had been told by an instructor on my course that some people would have given an arm or leg to be able to be a police driver. I'm not sure about that and I always saw it as a huge responsibility which could easily become a heavy burden if things went wrong as they sometimes did. A colleague overtook a queue of traffic waiting to turn right but the driver at the front of the queue hadn't seen him so turned into his path and he crashed into her. She was elderly and received a broken collar bone, and my colleague was given three points on his own licence after the matter had been investigated.

On the other hand there was nothing more exciting than arriving quickly at an incident having been able to skip through red traffic lights and with queues of traffic parting to make way. It also helped me to realise the importance of the nature of the work we were doing and that we had been given special privileges by the law makers. To flout or abuse this power never entered my mind. I was grateful to be entrusted with the responsibility. Police driving is definitely one of the main things I miss having left the police force.

Police pursuits, however, were a different kettle of fish. I lived in fear of inadvertently ending up involved in one. I didn't have the confidence with the procedures we had been taught and was petrified that something would go wrong and I would be made a scapegoat. I had heard horror stories from different areas of the force. The one that really stayed with me was about youths who had gone over a bridge at high speed and hit a wall and all five of them had been killed outright. On that occasion the police had been about to pursue the suspect vehicle and had turned round in order to do so, but hadn't done anything to influence the crash. The suspects may have sped up because they saw the police vehicle, but how could the officers in any way be responsible for that? However, this type of tragedy was a very real fear for many officers.

Fortunately, as in the public order cases, there was a whole stream of officers who felt differently to myself and were very keen to be involved in any type of pursuit. In most cases a traffic vehicle would take over the pursuit at an early stage as they had more specialised training. One successful pursuit I recall was after there had been a smash and grab robbery from jewellery shops in central Brighton. A colleague heard the registration number of the vehicle as he was en route to the scene of the incident and he saw the suspect vehicle in traffic. He immediately began a pursuit which went through several towns at high speed and eventually the suspects ditched the vehicle in a field and were tracked down, and one was bitten by police dogs. Most of the jewellery was recovered.

Domestic violence was one area where we had to get it right. Whenever there was a domestic murder (fortunately quite rare in Sussex) every officer immediately searched their memory to see if they had ever attended the home address of the couple. It was the same with Child Protection cases, especially after incidences like "Baby P". It's easy to think that you would have handled it better had you been involved but the reality was that in busy stations officers had unmanageable workloads and every so often these types of cases were inevitable. Actually, I lived in fear of this whilst working in Child Protection, knowing that one day a case could be overlooked or a wrong decision made resulting in the death of a child. I prayed that it wouldn't be one of my cases and I wouldn't have to bear the devastating guilt and widespread condemnation when that happened.

Victimless prosecutions (taking a case to court without the support of the victim) for domestic violence cases were becoming more common. One day I saw a report of an incident that some of my staff had attended. The original report from some independent witnesses stated that they had seen a man shoving a woman's head up against some railings in the street and that he had then kicked her. For some reason the officers had not spoken to the witnesses at length but had instead spoken to the "victim" and her partner who had played down the incident and refused to speak any further about it. This was the end of the matter as far as the officers were concerned.

I knew it would cause conflict if I intervened as the officers considered the matter closed, but I also knew that we couldn't leave it there as it was a domestic violence case and the violence could escalate in the future. I asked my officers to re-attend the incident and take statements from the two witnesses. When I read the statements later, I was appalled at the levels of violence described by the witnesses. The suspect was arrested and later charged based on the independent evidence, and even though his partner gave evidence in his defence at court, he was convicted. Later we were told that this case had been highlighted as an example of how victimless prosecutions were possible and could be used to protect victims experiencing domestic violence without them having to cooperate and risking the wrath of the offender. Over-ruling officers in this way and asking them to re-investigate things was not something I enjoyed but it was a necessary part of being a supervisor.

As I gained confidence in my supervisory role, I often tried (and mostly failed) to address procedural matters that I felt were inefficient or just plain wrong. One of the most annoying procedures for sergeants is that every time a person dies and officers have attended, a supervisor must also attend to check everything. A doctor has to be called to certify death even if death is obvious. This was probably because there had been two cases in the last one hundred years where people considered to be dead were not and had woken up in trays in the morgue. Public services tended to react to this type of thing by trying to ensure their procedures were adapted to cover every eventuality.

So it was one day that I attended the scene of a report of an elderly man who had died. The dead man was bent over sitting on his sofa in his lounge and had clearly been dead for some time; rigor mortis had set in. However, when I asked for an undertaker to come, I was informed that a doctor had to attend first in order to certify death. This was necessary unless decomposition had begun or part of the body was detached! Then began a back and forth discussion lasting at least ten minutes during which I insisted that an undertaker was called straight away because the man was definitely dead, but the control room supervisor wanted a doctor to attend anyway to comply with procedure. I dreaded the embarrassment of a local doctor arriving, having been rudely interrupted from his work and ordered to attend our location, only to pronounce the obviously-dead man as "officially dead" and leave again.

I was reassured, however, on reading an article on the BBC News website that the English police procedures are not the craziest in the world. The Minister for Justice was being shown around prisons in the Democratic Republic of the Congo and was surprised not only to find humans in the cells awaiting their fate, but also a herd of goats. They were being charged with being sold illegally at the roadside. The Minister ordered their immediate release and blamed the local police whom he subsequently sent for "re-training" to avoid a similar occurrence. The journalist commented that the goats would no doubt be relieved at being spared the ordeal of a trial as conditions in jails in Congo are known to be poor! (BBC News)

# CHAPTER THIRTY-SEVEN

# The Worst Crash

The worst crash I was required to attend occurred on the A24 main dual carriageway. The initial call was for a man walking in the road, which was graded as a prompt response but not an emergency, as it wasn't initially known that it was on the dual carriageway. Two of my officers attended the incident but couldn't find anyone. I was listening to the police radio in the office when I heard the control room operator advising that they had received another call from someone stating that they had just "hit a pedestrian". On hearing this, I was straight out of the office and jumping into the nearest police car, urging the rest of my staff to do the same. On the way to the incident I could hear the frantic tones of my two officers who were looking for the man as they arrived on scene and began trying to manage the incident. One of the main dangers was that the main road was still open and although one lane of the carriageway was blocked, vehicles were still whizzing past them as they worked to stabilise the man on the road. It was only a matter of time before the incident turned into a double tragedy.

I saw the incident on the opposite side as I headed south along the A24. I immediately parked my vehicle across both lanes of the northbound carriageway, effectively closing the road. However, this was only a temporary solution as I needed to get to the incident to support my officers. I called on the radio for another officer to take over the road closure and within minutes someone arrived, allowing me to leave and head for the incident. The man was in a really bad way on our arrival, having been hit by several vehicles. One witness told us that he had been travelling along the southbound carriageway when he had seen the man sitting up in the road waving his arm before being hit by a vehicle. This witness was obviously in shock and hearing what he had seen shocked me as well.

When the ambulance staff arrived it was a relief as although we were doing our best to help the man, our medical knowledge was basic and it was obviously a case that needed urgent specialist intervention. I was surprised that the ambulance staff decided to treat the man on the road and by the length of time all of this took; we were there for several hours. During this time a family member rang the man's mobile phone and we found a card in his pocket from his close family members. This made the whole situation very difficult as this was clearly a man with a young family.

When the traffic officers arrived, they asked me to take an account from an elderly couple who were sitting in their vehicle near the scene. They had been driving one of the vehicles that had hit the man and we needed to establish what had happened. I got in the back of their vehicle expecting them to be upset, but they were more annoyed than upset and were asking why they had been told they couldn't leave and couldn't drive their vehicle home. I was a bit bemused by this as my vehicle would have been the least of my concerns if I knew I had just run someone over. But as I began talking to them and asking questions, it began to dawn on me that they hadn't a clue what had happened. Then the awful moment came when the realisation kicked in and one of them turned to me and said in a voice full of anguish, "You mean we hit a person?" before both of them dissolved into tears and began mumbling about how they had thought it was just a pile of debris in the road. I struggled to contain my own emotion as I realised how dreadful this must have been for them. Later we took them home as their vehicle had to be seized for forensic testing.

The medical helicopter finally arrived and the man was airlifted to hospital. After cleaning up the scene, another staff member and I drove silently back to the police station, but on the way back we received a call from our control room informing us that, sadly, the man had died at the hospital. All of us who had been involved in this incident were affected by it and I found it especially difficult as it brought back memories of my brother's accident. Later we had a meeting to discuss what had happened as a way of moving on, but this type of incident is not something that is ever forgotten.

# CHAPTER THIRTY-EIGHT

# Country Policing

After a while at Horsham, I was given the opportunity to move to the more rural area of Steyning which also covers Pulborough. I liked this idea as it placed me closer to my home in Findon Valley and I thought it would give me more driving experience as there were a lot of country roads. I was also looking forward to the change from town policing and the quieter pace of life in the country.

The first thing to mention is that working at Steyning was nothing like I thought it would be and that it definitely wasn't quieter or more relaxed than Horsham. For one thing, it took longer to get to emergencies, which sometimes resulted in routine incidents escalating and pending colleagues arriving as backup. It was also sometimes awkward as I had grown up in Storrington, which was within my new area, so inevitably I encountered individuals who knew either me or my family, as my father had also lived in the area all his life. Sometimes this was an advantage as I discovered one day when some "members of the travelling fraternity" (gypsies) who had refused to speak to me or my colleagues changed their tune immediately on hearing my surname and became very cooperative and willing, but this wasn't always the case.

On several occasions I found myself fearing for my personal safety whilst dealing with public order situations in and around Storrington. It was (as one of my Horsham staff remarked) as if we were dealing with a different breed of criminal. He made the comment after being confronted by a gang of youths when he was dealing with an incident. When he threatened to arrest one of them if they didn't comply with his instructions, he was informed that he was just one against all of them and was unlikely to win. Such blatant threats of violence were fortunately rare in our line of work and so all the more shocking when they were made.

During another incident there was Captor spray and batons galore as we struggled to control a man whom we needed to arrest for a domestic assault. We felt compelled to withdraw quickly once he was under control as half of the community had suddenly appeared outside their houses and were walking menacingly towards us. I wouldn't have wanted to rely on the law that states that if a police officer is in trouble and asking for assistance, you have to go to his aid, in the middle of this crowd!

Of course, it wasn't always serious and dangerous. We had some fun, too, and most of the time at Steyning this came in the form of various "animal" related incidents that are the bane of any police officer's life working in a rural police station. We were frequently called to deal with escaped cows, sheep and horses, with no real role on arrival other than to keep eyes on them and report their whereabouts to the nearest farmer. My colleague remarked that he didn't understand why people called the police as we couldn't do anything more than the person who had called us. It was as if people thought we had magical powers to deal with any and all incidents that crossed their paths.

We were also called to deal with the many incidents of "road kill" in and around the area, usually in the form of deer. I recall one evening having attended such an incident, getting out of the police vehicle which my colleague had temporarily parked on a blind bend, and struggling single-handedly to drag an enormous deer from the middle of the road whilst not getting run over in the process. My colleague had to remain in the vehicle for safety as it might be necessary for him to lurch forward at any moment if any vehicles approaching from the rear were unable to stop in time. After a few attempts, another officer was summoned and managed to remove the offending carcass from the road to the grass verge with a spade.

The strangest incident involving a deer was one that occurred at 3am on the dual carriageway. We had received a call about the animal and had spent a considerable amount of time driving slowly along the deserted highway with our full beam on, searching for the alleged hit-and-run victim. Eventually we found it and stopped in the road. Two of us approached the animal, leaving our headlights on to allow us to work, but then neither of us wanted to touch it as it looked like it was in remarkably good form for a "dead" deer and I was afraid that it might suddenly come back to life and either scare me out of my wits or hoof one of us as it made good its escape.

My irrational fear of the unknown struck again but this time it was contagious as we both stood at a distance in the road and wondered what to do. Then the ridiculous nature of our predicament hit me as I realised how it might look if anyone were to drive past at this moment with two police officers standing in the unlit road staring at the carcass of a deer, seemingly afraid to approach it.

In the end we called a third officer to join us and he suggested we get a tool from the boot of his car to poke the animal and make sure it was actually dead. On carrying out this action and achieving the necessary confirmation, another officer and I took hold of two of the legs of the definitely dead animal and began swinging it slowly back and forth, gaining momentum as we did so. Then after a short time, we counted, "one, two, three," and swung the animal into the ditch at the side of the road.

Another time, part of my sergeant duties involved looking after a stray dog that had been brought to the police station by a member of the public who had found it in the street. I was pleased that the dog was friendly but paranoid that my inspector might turn up and chastise me for allowing the animal to enter the station as it created havoc racing around and crashing into things. In the end I had to keep one officer free to supervise the dog at all times until its owner arrived to collect it.

I was also caught off guard one day when I recognised a dog that had appeared with its owner (a twenty-year-old girl) in the backyard of Steyning police station. I couldn't work out where I knew her from until finally she reminded me that she had attended my home address a few months previously in answer to an advertisement for lodgers. We had decided not to go ahead with the arrangement in the end after we had left the dog in my house for ten minutes and when we returned he had ripped my carpet to pieces having been so desperate to get out. I was also relieved about my earlier decision on learning that the girl was at Steyning Police Station because her ex-boyfriend, whom she had assured me would be no trouble, had assaulted her and threatened to kill her.

Working at Steyning we had to deal with the regular policing of the hunt activities and suddenly I was thrust into a different world as I had to learn every last detail about fox hunting laws. Having no firm opinion either way, although I don't like cruelty to animals, I found myself often infuriated by both sides as I witnessed them deliberately provoking each other and moving as close to the line as they possibly could without crossing it, or on some occasions crossing it and then expecting the police to step in immediately. Both sides were using us for their own ends, or deliberately trying to trap us into saying the wrong thing on camera, or tricking us into arresting them for minor infringements and then later suing us for unlawful arrest. I didn't envy the courts having to sort out the many incidents that made it that far and often resented the huge amounts of time and money that were spent policing these activities. It was just part of the job working in that area and luckily I didn't have to supervise many such activities.

Continuing tales from the lighter side, I had never been a stickler for procedures (as I'm sure you have gathered) unless I could see the purpose of them. As such, I wasn't interested in harassing my staff about their general appearance and other such matters unless I was advised to deal with a particular issue by the powers that be. Work-wise, on the other hand, I was pretty strict and had high standards which I expected my staff to follow.

Learning the location and procedures for the station alarms should have been a priority on arriving at a new station, especially one such as Steyning where there were often few or no other sergeants for miles around. Unfortunately, this had slipped into my "non-essential" box so that when I was alone in the station one day, I had no idea what to do when the intruder alarm went off. Oh, and I failed to mention that the reason the alarm went off was because I had opened the back door and didn't know the security code to deactivate the alarm.

Obviously, I was hoping to keep this embarrassing state of affairs to myself and thought this would be pretty easy to do, until I contacted one officer after another only to be told they didn't know it either. Seemingly the only officer with the now essential knowledge was busy dealing with an incident and wouldn't be free for some time. My now red cheeks became scarlet as I was contacted by the control room to advise me about the alarm as I was the duty supervisor for the area and they wanted me to check it out. They were unable to give me the reset code over the phone so in the end one of my officers had to attend with blue lights flashing to check that I wasn't under duress and to reset the alarm. I didn't hear the last of that for a while.

On another day I was again alone in the police station but was frantically busy with all types of urgent matters, when I received a call from the front desk. It appears a member of the public had walked into Steyning Police Station to complain about an incident that was occurring just outside the station in the street and they wanted an officer to go and sort it out. On hearing it was a road rage type incident, at first I said that there was no one to deal with it immediately as all of my officers were busy and I was heavily committed at the station. However, this wasn't satisfactory to the member of the public who soon came back again to request attendance. The lady in the front office had made it clear that there was only one sergeant in the station and that I was working on other urgent matters, but the person was persistent. In the end I went outside to resolve the matter, fearing that things might get out of hand and that I would be criticised for not securing a peaceful outcome, having been requested to attend. I was not happy though and was not wearing my usual patient smile.

Feeling irritated and with a "this had better be good" attitude, I walked the twenty metres from the front of the station to where the incident was meant to be happening, but on arrival saw only two vehicles facing each other in a narrow street. There was no noise and no problem as far as I could see but the road was too narrow for both vehicles to pass so one of them was obviously going to have to back up and let the other one through. I assumed there was more to it than this and approached the driver nearest to me to ask what had happened. As soon as I realised that this was just a case of stubbornness and that the incident was nothing more than I had initially observed, I exploded with annoyance and said to the first driver, "Don't you think your local police sergeant has got better things to do than deal with this? Obviously, one of you will have to back up as you can't pass each other because the road is too narrow. Did you really need me to come and tell you that? For goodness sake, you are both adults." Then I walked across to the other driver and as he opened his mouth to give his side of the non-story, I let forth with a similar spiel, then stalked back to the police station, not bothering to check whether they were following my advice, leaving both of them open-mouthed at my rudeness. Clearly, this was not something that I made a habit of, but should the police really be called to deal with something like that?

The most mysterious incident that occurred at Steyning was one night when I was driving with a colleague along the main road towards Storrington. We drove past a man walking out of Storrington on the pavement. I thought that maybe we should stop and have a chat with him as it was late and he was heading towards an area with no residential houses. I looked in my rear view mirror just in time to see the man dash behind our car across the road and then dive into the hedgerow. Of course this caused me immediately to back up the road but by the time we had got back to the location, the man had vanished. After a few minutes of fruitless searching, we asked for a police dog to attend to see if he could find a track.

After a while the dog and his handler tracked the man and only reappeared after several hours, advising that they had, unfortunately, lost the track. However, they had tracked the man for a long time and reported that during his desperate bid for freedom he had lost one expensive trainer and an iPod or MP3 player. He had also plunged into a fairly deep pond and made his way through very thick undergrowth which would have required some determination. He had gone a very long way over difficult terrain in the pitch black. I wanted to carry out forensic tests on the shoe in case we had reports the following day of crime from the area the man had come from. I waited eagerly for reports to emerge, but when no such calls were forthcoming we had to put the matter to bed. I wonder to this day what the man had done that was worth risking a serious injury for; I just had to remind myself of the age old police phrase when we lost a prisoner or court case: "He'll come again." And they nearly always did.

# CHAPTER THIRTY-NINE

# Pastures New

I mentioned in an earlier chapter that I had always struggled with shift work and never felt properly adjusted to it. A while earlier the force had abandoned the popular shift pattern that had been successfully operating for many years and adopted a new pattern which chopped and changed our shifts so much that people began experiencing health issues. It was impossible to attribute the issues to the new shift pattern directly, but my staff certainly began complaining that they were constantly tired and having domestic problems that they attributed to the change.

I also began to feel very unwell at times and recall at around 3am on night shifts being so desperate to go to sleep that I would have happily paid £1,000 to anyone who had the ability to allow me to go home early. Fortunately, the few people I shared this shift with didn't have the power to make it happen so the money remained safely in my bank account. I was feeling totally exhausted to the extent that it was affecting my quality of work and my relationships with staff and others at my station.

Over the years I had gone through fitness spurts (as most of us do) where I had joined a gym and gone at it wholeheartedly for a while only to give up and then begin again after a few months. At this time I was playing squash and netball regularly, as well as cycling, walking and several times a year heading to Wales with a group of Christian friends for some pretty serious hiking activities. On these trips I usually remained in the lead group, despite sometimes (usually halfway up a particularly gruelling mountain) wondering why on earth I was doing this in my spare time.

Therefore, I was surprised one day whilst participating in a group cycling trip to find myself at the back and struggling to keep up. Of course, I blamed my fitness levels and was humiliated as I had a reputation to maintain. I ended up being physically unable to continue the journey and had to swallow my pride and take a downhill shortcut back to the car park. On arrival, I crawled into the back of one of our cars and promptly fell asleep in the middle of the afternoon. After that I slept for the entire weekend, all of which is now a blur in my mind. Something was clearly wrong.

On returning home I had some blood tests and was informed that I had an underactive thyroid. This was something which I had never heard of but which apparently was going to require me to take medication every day for the rest of my life and allowed me free prescriptions on the NHS for all of my ailments, also for life! I gathered from this that it must be serious but it took me a while to accept that I had a health problem; initially I persisted in believing that my energy problems were my own fault due to a lack of physical exercise. I tried to continue as normal with my shifts but became more and more exhausted and, as a result, increasingly irritable.

Bizarrely or providentially (depending on your perspective) at this exact moment in time, Sussex Police decided to implement a new policy to allow unpaid leave for up to six months. The reason: they were strapped for cash due to government cutbacks. The criteria: very flexible. I applied immediately and was granted the six months unpaid leave I had requested, effective immediately. During my illness, I had begun to wonder whether I could tolerate another twenty or so years within the police force and so the plan was not only to use this time to rest and recuperate but also to look for another job or career, which was permitted within the career break policy as long as we didn't actually begin our new jobs whilst still on career break. Even before the new policy was put in place, some staff members had found the general principle difficult to understand, as they were caught painting windows and doing other paid work whilst on long-term sick leave from the police!

I hadn't definitely decided that I wouldn't return to the police at the end of the six months but I was hoping to find another option as the shift work was killing me one piece at a time. I prayed that God would clearly direct me and then began the job hunt. I researched current jobs nationwide, sending applications and emails galore with little or no response. In addition to the police related jobs, I applied for many jobs in full-time Christian work, always within the UK, of course, as I had no desire or plan to travel abroad for work. For all of this activity, I didn't get a single request for an interview! Some of the jobs I had applied for were one third of my salary in the police and didn't have any application requirements. This frustrating and demoralising period totally humbled me as I started to realise that I might not be the world's most desirable employee having spent almost ten years with Sussex Police!

When I had picked myself up from my wretched heap on the floor and took time to pray, I realised that God might just be answering my original prayer for direction in a way that I wasn't expecting. In my experience, this is how God tends to work but it never fails to catch me out. Sometimes I feel like a child making the same mistake and learning the same lessons over and over again. Subconsciously I had limited my job search to a paid position in the UK. I didn't want to rely on others for financial support and I had justified remaining in the UK for health reasons.

It was only when I completely removed these unnecessary barriers that the way forward started to become clear. I began checking the vacancies at the various Christian missionary organisations on the Internet and my search landed on Operation Mobilisation (OM). In 2007, just three years before, I had gone on a Short Term Mission with this organisation to London. The mission had been very Gospel focused and had really challenged me. In fact, on my return I decided to commit one week of my annual leave from the police every year to mission and I had faithfully done this. I had heard of OM's ships that sail around the world but didn't know that much about them. The idea of being on a ship appealed to me straight away so I looked up the information on the website.

Then I made a tentative enquiry by phoning the OM office, but at that stage I was still worried that I might be pursuing my own agenda without realising it. This was totally irrational as I was praying all along that God would close any wrong doors and open the right ones. He was, and is, more than capable of that so I really had nothing to fear. I had a meeting with my church pastor who was supportive and encouraged me to apply to OM Ships if I believed God might be leading me in this direction.

I realised that if I was going to become a missionary, I would need to save up some money. I hadn't worked for four months and still had two months left of my career break from Sussex Police. There was no provision in the career break policy for an early return from a break. I decided that there was no harm in asking, and so in March 2011, I phoned the Human Resources department, expecting my request to be denied straight away. I highlighted the fact that I was planning to take another two year career break later in the year so the force would be saving money further down the line. I was still surprised and grateful when they said yes and agreed to let me come back to work full-time straight away and to work up until the date I would potentially leave.

So in April 2011, after gathering more information and heading back to work, I applied to OM Ships. I began to get excited about the prospect of going but still wasn't sure if it was really right. Then I was informed that I would need to attend a preparation weekend and that the next vacancy was in July. The next intake for the ship was in August so it would be unlikely that I would be ready in time to go on the ship as I hadn't yet submitted an application or had an interview or even made a firm decision that it was the right way forward. Then someone unexpectedly dropped out of the preparation weekend in April and I was able to take their place.

At the end of April, I travelled to the OM base in England. I prayed that at this weekend God would make His will very clear to me, and He did. I was really impressed with the focus on evangelism during the weekend and although I didn't agree with everything that was said, there was enough common ground for me to move forward. I submitted my application then and there.

As I moved further into the planning stages and received more details of life on the ship, Logos Hope, I mentally prepared myself for a tough two years. I was interviewed by OM and officially accepted but was then informed that there was no space on the ship and that I would have to wait until the following August to join. I realised that this wouldn't work as I had informed the police that I would be taking a career break for two years from August and my application was already being processed. I informed OM that I was willing to go anywhere in the world but that I must go in August. OM searched their vacancies and advised me that I could go to the war-torn country of Afghanistan instead of the ship. I agreed that I would be willing to go to Afghanistan but in my heart I knew that this wasn't what would happen as, by this time, I was sure God would make a way for me to go on the ship. My contact at OM UK said she would contact the ship officially about me anyway, even though they had already said that there was no space. Thankfully, she called me back later that day with the exciting news that Logos Hope had accepted me to join their team in late August 2011.

# CHAPTER FORTY

# A Step Backwards?

Eanwhile, back at work for Sussex Police, people were surprised to see me as they had expected that I would find a new job and move on during my temporary break. I felt like a bit of a failure as I had already said my goodbyes, received some cards and farewell gifts, and now I was back. I had even given away bits of my uniform which it was now necessary to reclaim. But it was really a great time to explain to people what I was going to be doing and why. My colleagues were stunned and listened to my plans with incredulity.

I know that many of them thought that I was a "good person" and doing a "good thing" by sacrificing two years of my life to go abroad and help people. Most people focused on the aid and charity work aspect and few understood that I was really going to share my faith with people, as well as helping them practically. Indeed many people may have been offended or less interested if they had really listened to what I was going to be doing. Those who were more astute did ask tricky questions like, "What makes you think that you have the right to go and try to change someone else's religion?" and, "Isn't it arrogant to go into someone else's country and tell them what they should believe?" These were tough questions but showed that people were interested.

The simplistic answer to these questions is that logically there can only be one true faith as the different faiths are made up of components that are fundamentally opposed to each other. If Christianity is true then other faiths must be false and vice versa. I often hear people saying things like, "What's true for you may not be true for me!" but this is really an illogical statement because if something is true, it is true for everyone. In the Bible, God claims to be the one true God and I believe that the decision a person makes about this claim determines their final "forever" destination.

Other people at work thought "going on a cruise" and "experiencing foreign travel" was a great idea and were jealous. I didn't go to great lengths to explain to these people how wrong they were as I knew that whatever I said, the images of sandy beaches and cocktails had already been ingrained in their minds and would not easily be removed.

Whilst I had been away, the whole police force had been re-structured to allow for government changes and my Sergeant post at Steyning had been filled. So I was placed in a pool of officers with no official frontline role, known as a "Reserve Team" or as the many disgruntled officers within it called it, "the loser pot". The idea was that eventually all of these officers would be moved out of the team and into permanent posts across the force. Most of the officers in this pool didn't want to be there for one reason or another and it was extremely hard to boost morale. I could totally understand this as my only motivation at this time was the fact that I would be leaving soon and that I was really there to earn a bit of money for my future outside of the police. Being in the team did feel a bit like being cast aside, and if I felt like that having just come back from a break, I can't begin to imagine how those who had been working in permanent posts felt when they were rejected in favour of others within their teams. It was also hard to build a rapport within the team as over time officers were removed and sent to permanent posts, which was great for them but hard for those left behind. It reminded me a bit of the kids who are always picked last for sports competitions at school.

My being placed in this team only increased my reputation for station hopping as I was now stationed at Burgess Hill for a few months. It was a long drive but I was really grateful to the force for allowing me to come back unexpectedly and at short notice, so I didn't complain. I did request a transfer to Worthing, though, and was allowed to do this later down the line.

Back at Worthing I spent a few weeks in the Response Investigation Team supervising cases that came in to Worthing custody centre. It was here that I witnessed a colleague sergeant saving the life of our inspector who had choked on the stone of a piece of fruit. She successfully carried out the Heimlich manoeuvre on him to everyone's relief as he had been turning blue and gasping desperately for air.

After this I was sent to Littlehampton, my ninth station in as many years; it seems I never could quite reach ten. I was to work on a Special Project for a detective inspector involving carrying out research for a planned future project for the Child Protection Department in which I had previously worked. During this time I also became involved in working with the Major Crime Branch on an investigation into a possible "shaken baby" death case.

These difficult few months, where I felt as if I were moving from pillar to post without a firm foundation, ended on a high note. As I left CPT on my last day, the detective inspector I had been working for asked to see me. He said that he was really grateful for all of the good work I had done over the few weeks I had worked for him as I had done exactly what he had asked for. He added that if I came back to the force after my two year career break and needed a good word put in to get into a desired post, that I should contact him and he would be happy to provide the recommendation. I knew even at this stage that there was little chance I would come back but hearing the sincere words of praise from a senior officer and the open door should I choose to return was a great encouragement.

So, after those four additional and painfully slow months, I walked away from my final duty on that final day, feeling a strange mixture of slight fear, nostalgia, freedom and excitement, but really having no idea how the next few years would pan out. I trusted that God knew, and had a plan and purpose for my life, and that was enough for me.

# Epilogue

In September 2013, I returned from my two year stint on board the Logos Hope ship a changed person, and without qualms immediately resigned from my post as Police Sergeant in order to follow God's call to head to the Philippines as an independent missionary evangelist. The procedure seemed to be straightforward, until I was contacted by the police about the whereabouts of my warrant card (police badge) for which I had already searched high and low and knew that I didn't have. Potentially this could have had serious consequences and allowed anyone inclined to do so to impersonate a police officer.

The saga ended when amongst the four boxes of personal items that I had to my name (having sold everything to go to the Philippines) I found a pot containing a lot of random keys. One of the keys which I didn't recognise had a tag with a number attached to it. On the off-chance that it meant something I contacted the police and asked if they had any lockers with this specific number and told them roughly where my last locker had been. Soon after this I received a message advising me that the administration department had "broken into" my locker and discovered my warrant card and many other items which they were more than willing to dispose of. A happy ending all round.

So, three years down the line, did I do the right thing? Do I miss being a police officer? Would I go back in time and do things differently? Do I regret giving up the salary, the stable job and the police pension?

The most important thing in all of this was to determine what God's will was for my life. I felt that God was drawing me out of the police and preparing me for something different but I needed to be sure. God provided the confirmation that it was right for me to go onto the ship in several ways. One of these was that the lodgers with whom I had been sharing my house decided to move out. They had paid a deposit on another house and their moving date was fast approaching. However, at the last minute the other side in their arrangement pulled out and they decided to stay in my house, taking over the tenancy and paying my mortgage. Even my lodgers, who at that stage were non-believers (they have since become Christians) said that they felt as if things were being taken out of their hands (directed from above).

Because of the clear confirmation of my calling, I left my job knowing that God would protect and help me during my journey. I found that although I was unsure of myself when I was making the initial decisions, I had to take small steps of faith and that these steps were what opened the bigger doors. The experiences I had on the ship, particularly whilst in the Philippines, convinced me that God had prepared this specific path for me and that I had made the right decision in leaving the police.

Now, even though I'm sure I made the right decision, of course there are aspects of police work that I miss. Mostly I miss the people; I miss the camaraderie and friendships that develop within police teams who spend so much time together dealing with difficult incidents. I miss knowing what is really going on locally rather than just what is reported in the media. I miss being a sergeant; I miss supervising incidents, making decisions and managing people. I miss encouraging and motivating a team of people and seeing the results of that; I miss teasing my staff about their spelling and grammar (you know who you are). I miss being a detective; I miss the real detective work that occasionally hit my desk; I miss attending court for a case into which I have put a lot of work, hearing the judge's profound comments and getting a good result for the victim. I miss attending the funnier and more bizarre incidents, then relating the stories and laughing about them afterwards, and I definitely miss the police driving!

However, I don't miss the terrible shift patterns and the night shifts that made me feel like death; I don't miss the conflicts with staff, supervisors and all manner of people over incidents, practices and policy. I don't miss dealing with sudden death, serious road crashes and all incidents where someone has been seriously injured or killed. I don't miss the diversity training courses, or any training courses for that matter! I don't miss the salary, job security or pension benefits (honestly). I don't miss the weight of responsibility that was heavy at times; I don't miss the meddling of the politically correct brigade who lurk somewhere in every station seeking opportunities to take people down for expressing their opinions. I don't miss struggling for change and often being unable to deliver; I don't miss the frustrations of working within a set framework and a fixed way of doing things that wasn't always efficient.

Being a police officer and specifically a detective had been my childhood dream and this ambition was realised during my time with Sussex Police. The roles I undertook kept me busy, interested and challenged for varying lengths of time, but I tended to get itchy feet and begin thinking that there must be more to life; hence the many departmental changes and roles. At that stage I never would have considered leaving the police as it was my chosen career and I fully expected to complete my thirty years of service. Returning to my Christian faith in God in 2005 partially filled the hole in my life and changed my perspective in relation to my work. For a time I was able to settle down and serve as a police officer knowing that I was not only accountable to my colleagues and the public, but also to God for my attitude and actions at work.

However, largely due to the lifestyle I had lived whilst away from God and the black hole of hopelessness I had found myself in, the desire to reach out to others with the hope I had found in Jesus was always very strong. God knew that in 2005 I wasn't ready to head for the mission field or to move into full time Christian service. My ties to the police were too strong and I still had many things to learn about life and my relationships with others. God's timing really is perfect as he used those years to draw me out of the police and to prepare me for a completely different mission and calling. The unthinkable, leaving my stable job and career, became the "maybe as a last resort" and later "the only possible option" as He changed my priorities and reminded me of the importance of reaching out to lost souls still in darkness. He showed me that whilst I could continue to witness to my colleagues and to a lesser extent those I was dealing with through my work, I would only be truly free to really share if I gave up everything and followed His call to become a full-time Christian missionary.

As you can probably imagine, the last few years as a missionary in Asia have been very different to the first season of my life as a police officer in England, but God has been consistently faithful and gives me the courage and determination to continue day by day. I am excited about the many opportunities here in the Philippines to share His help and hope with many people caught in sinful vices and struggling with the effects of poverty. The cultures may be vastly different but the root of the human problem is always the same: sin. Therefore the only true solution is also the same: Jesus.

Jesus said, "I am the light of the world; whoever follows me will never walk in darkness but will have the light of life." (John 8:12)

You can learn more about what I am doing now at our charity website:

**olongapochristianhelpandhope.btck.co.uk**

Or, if you prefer, you can read my first book, "They're Rugby Boys, Don't You Know?" to learn about my initial experiences as a missionary whilst working amongst a group of street teenagers addicted to solvents in the Philippines.

# Natalie's Personal Story

I became a Christian at a young age primarily due to having been raised in a Christian home and being surrounded by Christianity. As a teenager there were times when I was really serious about my faith. But there were also times when I became distracted from God and I wasn't really building a personal relationship with Him. During a more serious faith phase at the age of seventeen, I was baptised by full immersion, but just six weeks later fell away from God in a dramatic fashion.

I subsequently spent six years immersed in the "party lifestyle", succumbing to many activities and bad habits that sought to replace God, including an abundance of alcohol, cigarettes, gambling, and the regular watching of violent films or horror movies. I moved from one non-Christian relationship to another in an attempt to find the happiness that eluded me. I became more and more miserable, attempting to ignore God but knowing deep down that He was really there and that I was under His judgement because of my lifestyle choices.

I began a course in Law and Criminology at Sheffield University in 2000, but dropped out after just six weeks to join Sussex Police, thereby fulfilling a childhood dream. In 2002, my younger brother James (who was a Christian) was tragically killed in a car accident at the age of just eighteen. My parents clung to their Christian faith at this time, but I became angry with God for allowing this to happen and resented Christians for judging my lifestyle.

In April 2005, after many other problems and a long struggle, I faced up to the fact that I was miserable and that my life was a total mess. I had recently witnessed my younger sister, Lauren, going through a mini-version of the same struggles. I then saw the resulting contentment after God graciously called her back to Himself and Lauren repented and trusted in Him. I knew that I was carrying the heavy weight of my many sins around on my shoulders every day. I sometimes woke up at night in a terrified state, believing I was going

179

to hell because of the things I had done. I knew that God was waiting for me to repent my sins and turn back to Him, and that He had been patiently waiting for a long time. I lived in constant fear that time would run out and that I may have tested God's grace one too many times. Eventually, God brought me to the end of my resources. All I could do was cry out for His help. I said sorry to God for my many sins. I believed His promise that "everyone who calls on the name of the Lord will be saved"[4]. God, by His grace, planted true faith in my heart and I determined to live a new life before Him.

I abandoned my sinful vices immediately and began regularly attending my former church, Worthing Tabernacle. Two Bible verses became very important to me as a result of my experiences. The first is found in John 6:67-68: "'You do not want to leave too, do you?' Jesus asked the Twelve. Simon Peter answered him, 'Lord, to whom shall we go? You have the words of eternal life.'" (NIV) These verses remind me that seeking anyone other than Jesus is a total waste of time because He is the only one with the words of eternal life that can offer hope for the future. The second verse is from Mark 8:36: "For what shall it profit a man, if he shall gain the whole world, and lose his own soul?" (KJV) This sums up my life experience as I tried seeking happiness in the world but foolishly risked losing my soul in the process.

When I tell people my story, I am often asked, "How do you know it was God who brought you back to your faith and not just a decision you made and carried out through your own will and determination?" This is a good question. The truth is that before I returned to the Lord, I didn't have the strength or desire to give up my vices; I had tried many times to turn my life around and always failed. Although I saw the emptiness and meaninglessness of life without God, and the utter futility of daily life lived without a purpose, I was powerless to make the big changes I knew were necessary. I was so immersed in my sinful lifestyle that a new start seemed like an impossibility. Before God could help me, I had to accept that I needed His help, that I was totally dependent and reliant on Him to restore me, and that I couldn't change anything myself. True salvation occurs only when God changes a person's heart, allowing them to believe in Him. The Bible says in

---

[4] Romans 10:13 (NIV)

Matthew 19:26, "With man this is impossible, but with God all things are possible." (NIV)

God already had His hand on my life, due to my Christian upbringing, former beliefs and the fact that many people were praying for me regularly. God protected me from serious harm throughout this period and from serious long-term consequences. Looking back, I am so grateful to God for the mercy, grace and patience that He demonstrated towards me during my rebellion. The Bible says in Ephesians 2:8-9, "For it is by grace you have been saved, through faith – and this is not from yourselves, it is the gift of God – not by works, so that no one can boast." (NIV) This is my personal experience and all of the glory for the change in my life goes to God as I wasn't capable of turning my own life around.

I wouldn't be a true evangelist without explaining what it means to become a Christian and how you too can be free of your sin and reconciled to God to spend eternity in heaven with Him one day. During my last few years of missionary service, I was taught a tool to explain the Gospel. It has been effectively used by millions of people around the world.

It is called the "Wordless Book" and consists simply of five coloured sheets of paper or material each representing part of the message of salvation found in the Bible:

YELLOW

This represents heaven. Do you want everlasting life in heaven?

The Bible tells us that the streets in heaven are paved with gold. It also tells us that God is light and that in Him there is no darkness and that Jesus (God's only Son) is the light of the world. Heaven is God's dwelling place and the Bible also tells us that no man has ever imagined the wonderful things that God has prepared in heaven for those that love Him.

Heaven is forever.

BLACK

This represents sin. What is wrong with the world? More importantly, what is wrong with me?

Being honest, we need to face the bad news in order to see the value of the good news. The Bible says that all people have sinned and fall short of the glory of God and that the wages of sin is death.

God is holy and cannot have anything to do with sin. God is righteous and just and, therefore, cannot just overlook our sin and forgive us because this would make Him unjust. Our sin separates us from God permanently. All sinners are destined to spend an eternity in hell without God. Hell is a truly terrible place where people will long to die because of their torment but will be unable to do so. Hell is forever. This is the bad news.

## RED

This represents the blood of Jesus. Why did Jesus need to die?

God loved us so much that He provided a way of for us to be reconciled to Him and to escape the torments of hell. He sent Jesus, His only son, to live a perfect life here on earth. It was necessary for a penalty to be paid for our sin. Jesus' purpose in coming was to allow Himself to be sacrificed and punished on a cross in the place of all who believe that He died for them, and who put their trust in Him.

He died instead of them so that they could be free from the guilty sentence hanging over them because of their sin. He died on that cross and then rose from the grave just three days later, proving that He had defeated sin and death once and for all. Jesus' death acted as a bridge between guilty sinners and God, allowing all who trust in Him to be forgiven for their sins and to live in heaven forever with God.

## WHITE

This represents being washed clean from sin. How can be we sure of God's acceptance?

Think of your life as a white sheet. Every time you sin, even in a small way, a black stain is left on the sheet. When a person becomes a Christian and turns away from their sin, God promises them a new start. He says that he will remember their sins no more. When God looks at the life of a Christian, he sees only Jesus and His righteousness instead of the sin.

GREEN

This represents growth. How should this change my life?

All true Christians will grow spiritually over time. In order to grow, Christians should regularly read the word of God (the Bible), pray, attend a church, spend time with other Christians, and tell other people about Jesus and His sacrifice for them.

These things do not save people. There are no "divine scales" weighing good and bad deeds as a determining factor for entry to heaven or hell. No human can ever do enough good things to get to heaven, as the standard required is perfection; this is why Jesus had to die.

The things described here are the grateful response of a Christian who has been rescued from a life of sin and death and has been reconciled to God for a life of hope and an eternal future in heaven.

Please contact me if you would like further information.

# Related Books by the Publisher

### Below Me, the Clouds
### Ron Collard
### ISBN 978-1-907509-31-5

From a military career in the Royal Air Force to missionary work in the Missions Aviation Fellowship, Ron has many times experienced the exhilaration of climbing through solid cloud and breaking into a new world of sunshine and dazzling blue sky. His life has also been like that: living through clouds of war, fear, illness, disappointment, heartache, anxiety, failure and despair, but lifted above them by a Power outside of his limited being, yet discernible in history and in the rough and tumble of modern everyday life.

### Another Promised Land
### Paulette Jones
### ISBN 978-1-910197-12-7

Paulette Jones and her husband, a pilot in the Royal Air Force, share a special passion for French culture, customs and cuisine. They plan to build a Rest and Recuperation Centre in France for military personnel.

But when a mystery sickness takes hold of Paulette's life, her dreams and hopes are gradually stripped away. Eventually she finds herself alone in a small hamlet, unable to work, suffering intense pain and with many difficult questions.

Filled with humorous anecdotes and sharp insights about life in France, Paulette's testimony demonstrates how God can restore our lives – not only for our good but for the blessing of the many people we encounter along the way.